Claire Nahmad has published a number of books on healing, herbalism, magic, folklore and angel lore. She lives in North Lincolnshire, England.

Angel
Messages

The Oracle of the Birds

CLAIRE NAHMAD

WATKINS PUBLISHING
LONDON

Distributed in the USA and Canada by Sterling Publishing Co., Inc.
387 Park Avenue South, New York, NY 10016

This edition first published in the UK in 2010 by
Watkins Publishing, Sixth Floor, Castle House,
75–76 Wells Street, London W1T 3QH

1 3 5 7 9 10 8 6 4 2

Designed and typeset by Jerry Goldie

Printed and bound in China

Library of Congress Cataloging-in-Publication Data Available

ISBN: 978-1-906787-51-6

www.watkinspublishing.co.uk

For information about custom editions, special sales, premium and
corporate purchases, please contact Sterling Special Sales
Department at 800-805-5489 or specialsales@sterlingpub.com

Contents

Introduction 1

The Bird of the Soul 5

How to Use the Oracle 10

The Oracle of the Birds 17

Appendix 1 – The Story of The Hawk of Achill: Its Links
with the Emerald Tablet and the Holy Grail 197

Appendix 2 – An Esoteric Interpretation of the
Story of the Yellow Dwarf 202

Appendix 3 – Brigid of the Isles 205

Index 210

To
ANN NAPIER,
'half angel and half bird',
this book is respectfully
dedicated.

Introduction

After the release of my book, *Summoning Angels*, I was delighted to learn from its readers that interest in a complete bird oracle had been generated by the inclusion of a partial one within that volume. I am pleased to offer this book, dedicated solely to the mysterious 'Language of the Birds', as an extended exploration of the spiritual meaning conveyed by different species of birds and the symbolic messages they bring to us.

The Language of the Birds was also known as the Green Language. It was associated with a sacred stone known as the Emerald Tablet, into whose mystical molecular complexity it is said that all the divine knowledge that God vouchsafed to the Earth was miraculously inscribed. The Green Language comprised the secret speech of the medieval and Renaissance occultists, used to express esoteric knowledge in a way that concealed it from the ignorance of the masses. Its concepts are derived from cosmic and divine truth, and there is a literalness in its name which refers to the ancient belief that birds are wisdom-keepers, couriers of sublime secrets and messengers of the Divine. It is a language rich in symbolism, whose complexity and intricacy never override its innate poetic simplicity.

Indeed, its simplicity is often so distilled and refined that it seems to source its images in a childlike perception enshrining fairytale, dream and magic. When the 13th-century alchemist Michael Scot taught that honey falls from the air into flowers and is then collected by the bees, he was not being whimsical and unscientific. He was in fact referring, via potent symbols, to closely guarded secrets regarding the distinction between the true and the false Ark of the Covenant, and the vital connection between the human soul, the bee and our planetary life-support systems.

The 'honey in the air' is the divine gold of the spirit that enters us through our breath when we attune ourselves to the 'God-breath' or the 'Mother-breath', which is simply a method where each breath is imaginally drawn through the heart so that we enter the sanctified realm within ourselves. This quiet, spiritually attuned breathing brings cleansing and purity to our perception, and banishes the perceptual distortions caused by material existence. Via this 'God-breathing', the honey or divine gold falls into the 'flowers', which symbolize our chakra system – those points in the body (the ductless glands) where the physical is conjoined to the worlds of the spirit. Once the divine gold is active within the chakras, the 'bees', or the components of the soul, can collect it and, by alchemical process, transform the soul and the spirit (the honey) into an integrated essence – a realized individual – which can in turn nourish others with its sweetness or love.

The bees and the birds have always been linked in popular conception, and it is noteworthy that, as the Earth's bee population mysteriously diminishes, so too does that of many species of birds. It is time to embrace holistically these divine messengers once again, to call them back to us through a renewed recognition of our kinship, so that regeneration might occur at every level of life. When the birds assume again their rightful place in our consciousness, we will no longer allow them to decline and die.

The strange and beautiful language associated with birds (the Green Language of the occultists) is also of interest to those who love angels and seek their friendship, because its origins and inspiration belong to a yet more sublime, angelically inspired Language of the Birds, delivered to the Earth by Enoch, the great mage.

To examine the deepest origins of this language, we need to understand the bloodline that descended from Lilith, the symbol of ascension. Lilith was reviled in ancient manuscripts, but a revision of her history reveals her more accurately as a sacred bequeather of life, exalted love, and joy. She was human, but enshrined divinity within her. The queen of Sheba was of her royal bloodline, together with other prominent women of goddess status who also shared a very strange characteristic belonging to Lilith – their legs were purported to be scaly and feathered, and their feet were claws.

If we think of the evolutionary transformation of dinosaurs into planetary birdlife, we can derive from this odd legend the mythopoeic idea of the serpent, creature of wisdom (Lilith was portrayed in later mythology as a fearful serpent, whereas this creature was deeply venerated in the civilization from which she arose) actively becoming the bird, creature of ultimate ascension and freedom. Lilith holds the secret of how we, as human souls, may collectively ascend, and her secret, despised by the later patriarchal traditions which sought different values, is connected with the sacredness of birds and their hidden language.

Lilith's daughter Luluwa married Cain (son of Eve) and this ancient king and queen are cited on ancient Sumerian clay tablets as the designated guardians of the Emerald Tablet, whose descendants would have inherited its knowledge. Their son, Enoch, was blessed and instructed by Luluwa and Lilith. It was his lifetime's work to transcribe the speech of the angels into sounds that resonated with human hearing and understanding. In several of the ancient manuscripts that were excluded from the Old Testament, it is reported that Enoch nearly met his death many times whilst he performed this almighty feat, because he attuned himself to angelic utterances that, in their cosmic grandeur, atomize frail human consciousness. Luckily, the angels themselves managed to save Enoch's soul from exploding into 'flashing silver fragments more numerous than the stars' and steered him to perceptual safety.

When Enoch finally produced his *magnum opus*, it was found to consist of a series of sounds that correlated to birdsong, and it was generally agreed by both himself and his followers that, apart from the speech of the very mightiest of the angels who encompass universes in their inconceivable resonances, Enoch had managed successfully to deliver the Language of the Angels to humanity. It was transcribed further into sigils and symbols, and fitted into concepts of human language. This became the occultists' Language of the Birds.

Nevertheless, in its original state of pristine grace, Enoch's language was actually the Language of the Angels, and it was given forth as a lexicon of birdsong.

So it is believed that an intimate link exists between birdsong and the angels: a connecting system of transcendent weaving golden filaments that surpasses the common conception of alchemy to make the angelic Language of the Birds the supreme alchemical ideation that connects heaven and Earth. The magical Milky Way, eternally associated with winged angels and home-going souls, is called in Finland 'the Birds' Way'. It is the mysterious stairway to the spiritual worlds, trodden by shamans and mystics but available to all, if we are taught how to listen to birdsong and recognize the angelic messages that birds deliver to us.

It is my purpose within these pages to move towards fulfilling this mission, so that we can make the secret of the ancients our own.

The Bird of the Soul

*T*he Bird of Beautiful Song', reads an ancient text by an anonymous scribe – 'that is the Bird of the Soul.' To draw close to the birds in spirit, to listen with an open heart to their cascades of song and to attune the soul to their joyous outpourings, is a poignantly beautiful way to embrace the angelic streams of life. Through their association with the angels, birds can teach us of the hidden beauties and mysteries which are secreted within the human soul. They bring us teachings about our own soul and the soul of all creation. They bear messages from the heavenly worlds, and through their flight, their songs and their presence, they open a doorway to the spheres of the spirit and lift us in our light bodies up into airy heights of invigorating sweetness.

One way in which we can attune to these soul aspects, these special soul qualities that are concealed like buried treasure within us, is to listen so closely to the calls of the birds that we can begin to imitate them. It doesn't matter if you have no power of mimicry; just do your best and you will eventually receive a response. In my experience, birds are most responsive to our answering calls in the early evening, before the approach of twilight. Single strains of birdsong are much easier to identify at this time, and take on a melodious richness and poignancy which delights and awakens the heart-intelligence. It is then that we can enter into antiphony with them; with practice, taking care to keep our communion heart-centred, we will find that the birds call back in answer to us.

Half an hour spent in enjoying such a pastime will have a truly magical effect on all the subtle vehicles within us. We will feel centred in peace, and as if we can gaze into limitless worlds inside our soul which scintillate with an exquisite radiance. Our soul will unfold unearthly wings and teach us that no prison, no chains either mental or physical can ever contain or bind us. We will know that we are free.

We can take this freedom out into our everyday world and help others to feel it and express it, not of course by dumping our responsibilities, because a freedom that disrupts the liberty and well-being of others would soon lead us into a merciless captivity, but rather by showing that the thousandfold fetters which arise and try to hold us in petty bondage each day are powerless to restrict, confine and stifle our singing soul and our dancing spirit. In our innermost soul we are winged beings, and we should soar and glide each day of our lives.

The practice of listening to birdsong, of allowing ourselves the time and the stillness to do so, is crucial to the soul development and unfoldment that the birds offer us. It is important to remember that the heart is a listening organ – the very word 'ear' is contained within its letters. Our intuition – 'inner tuition' – is facilitated by the act of listening with, and listening via, the heart.

Throughout the autumn and the winter months, birdsong can be enjoyed for a few moments from an open door or window. As the spring advances towards early summer, sit out in your garden or walk in the woodlands just after dawn or in the peace of the evening. If you do not have a garden, seek out a quiet place where birds congregate. Listen to the sweet symphony of birdsong as the day opens or closes like a flower. Listen to it as a whole and then distinguish its individual notes, their sounds and spaces of silence, their vibrations low or high, blithe or purring.

Spiritual teachers, both earthly and ascended, tell us that birdsong is magical. We have seen how there is a deep connection between angels and birds, and that the language of the one reflects the language of the other. We might say that actual birdsong is a lower harmonic of the songs of the angels; and angel language is not simply a means of communication. It is the means by which, via the divine inflow from the great Source of all, creation in its entirety is harmoniously sung or spoken into being. Mythologies and religious texts worldwide refer at some point to this deeply mystical singing or 'Word' which breathes the universe into being. Although this power streams forth from the divine imagination of what we might call God or the Great Spirit, it is the angels themselves who minister to the manifestation of the divine imagination, creating evolving form and ensouling it with ever more beautiful and rarefied essence as that material form progressively becomes a perfected receptacle for such essence.

Within each member of humankind, it is said, the whole of the cosmos is reflected in microcosm. Therefore, these vibrations which so mysteriously create and bring into being are present in the depths of each human soul. The resonances of birdsong play upon this magical harp of Apollo or Orpheus within us and draw forth vibrations which, in turn, respond to sacred influences from the heavenly worlds. Our consciousness then becomes as the Holy Grail, a sanctified vessel which can be filled with divine life, with angelic emanations corresponding to the dancing ray from heaven in harmony with the particular notes of birdsong we are responding to. Within this etheric vessel lies the secret of creation itself, and we can recreate ourselves, our lives, and even our environment via its divine potency. When we receive such a blessing, we can fulfil the purpose of the angels by giving unstintingly of this divine force within our consciousness, and also protecting it from the ravages of those who, through ignorance, would destroy it.

Maud Gonne, the great love in the life of the visionary poet W B Yeats who saw in her spirit strong elements of both angel and goddess, could not bear to be without her songbirds. Although she was rootless and travelled constantly by train, she surrounded herself with cages full of birds, needing their life-affirming, soulful presence in spite of the practical inconvenience they represented. Her soul-mates were vital to her well-being. In order to celebrate the angel and the god within us, we too need to be constantly surrounded by the soul-energies of birds. We can ensure that we are by regularly attuning ourselves to the harmonies of birdsong and to the joy and mystery of their presence, seeking to understand them and their angel-inspired language.

Throughout myth and folktale, birds intervene dramatically in the life of human beings. In poetry and literature, their secret significance comes to light again and again. W B Yeats refers to them many times throughout his work. In 'Paudeen', he tells the story of his exasperation with a prosaic, small-minded shopkeeper 'until a curlew cried, and in the luminous wind, / a curlew answered'. It was borne to him that in the truth and the vision of the spiritual worlds, high above the confusion and distortions of the Earth, 'There cannot be…a single soul that lacks a sweet crystalline cry'; and the poet's heart was restored to the holistic vision of a world where all creatures sound their own note of beauty throughout creation.

And in 'A Memory of Youth', he tells how, although love had its earthly expression in the usual rapport between a man and a woman, which is enough for youth, its spiritual face or presence eventually became hidden away by 'a cloud from the north', or the colder climes of human nature; and how he and his lover would thus have been 'savagely undone' '…Were it not that Love upon the cry / Of a most ridiculous little bird / Tore from the clouds his most marvellous moon.'

Go profoundly inside the sound of birdsong and find the point of silence within its pulsations, the potent stillness beneath the notes. If, by an act of your spiritual will, you can exclude all invasive noise except these hallowed sounds and silences, you will begin to hear the symphony of life itself moving through your being, the songs of the angels themselves as they sustain creation in its forward motion, in its grand cycles and great sacred spiral. The birds can give you this gift of revelation. They can tear from the clouds of dimmed spiritual vision Love's 'most marvellous moon'. They can embody heavenly qualities with the sound of their songs and link you via the stairway of these sacred sounds directly to the heart of the Great Spirit.

In considering the birds and their songs in a spiritual light we will, no doubt, before long come across the point of view which informs us that birds squabble, steal, abandon, bully, fight and kill with the best of the earthbound species. This is true, of course; birds do belong to earthly communities which behave according to territorial and predatory instinct. Whilst ever the birds evolve within the physical and psychic patterns that currently belong to the Earth, this must be so. The birds cannot rise above biological necessity with regard to their earthly survival.

But there is a secret within the heart of nature which we need to discover and understand. It is that humanity itself holds the key to transposing the life forces so that they do not bring about suffering and oppression. When we as a planetary society truly rise above the dictates of our lower nature, which is rooted in the concept of the ego – the little defensive earthly self – and assume the raiment of our spiritual reality, then the breath of transformation will course through nature and bring into harmony those aspects of it which can seem so distressing. Yet this task is for us to fulfil. The angels and their earthly kinsfolk, the birds, ever seek to help us undertake this challenge. So it is not so much within the confines of biological necessity that we can touch upon the spiritual blessing the birds bring, as that which is ethereal and symbolical in their nature, those qualities of being that they express which transcend the pressures of earthly organization.

Nevertheless, in spite of 'biological necessity', we find that those very transcendent spiritual qualities swoop and hover over their earthly limitations. Stories abound concerning the depth of their love for their young, and mothers have been observed shielding their chicks in the nest from forest fires until both adult and nestlings have perished. Parent birds of both genders will feign injury to tempt away predators from their fledglings, and their distress is palpable when their offspring are stolen or destroyed, even when they are still unhatched. Their notes and trills when hatching their eggs or covering their young are infinitely tender and joyful, and many birds mate for life, expressing a constancy and loyalty which is rare among the human species. (See Sold for a Farthing by Claire Kipps, which tells the miraculous but true story of a sparrow which served its nation in the Second World War.)

Birds navigate by the stars and some undertake voyages as a yearly pilgrimage which would unnerve all but the stoutest of human hearts. The young swift will not touch the ground for three years after it leaves the nest, beggaring our achievements in aerodynamics. Their physical shape and colour, even their habits, have spiritual significance as well as their songs and their domain of air.

The notes of birdsong are akin to the angelic language as it was revealed to Enoch the prophet. Listen closely to birdsong and you will begin to receive angelic messages.

How to Use the Oracle

The Oracle of the Birds can be used in a number of ways. The art of bibliomancy can be employed by focusing simply and clearly on any particular question you have in mind, then opening the book with your left hand and allowing your right hand to rifle through the pages without looking directly at them until you sense an indication to halt. Wherever your forefinger alights is your pointer to the bird which will speak to your soul via the message it has to convey. Some users of bibliomancy simply open a book, and take their prophecy from the random page they thus alight upon.

Another method of divination involves calling upon our totem birds. The totem bird or animal is one whose spiritual consciousness, expressed through its appearance and behaviour, resonates in evocative attunement with our own soul and acts as guide, counsellor, healer, protector and catalyst upon our spiritual path. Whilst there is generally one overlighting totem bird for each human soul whose energies and inspiration are always present, there also exist a Bird of Night and a Bird of Day, each aligned to us individually, on which we can call for guidance. Your Bird of Day will usually be identifiable as your overlighting totem bird. The categories for each are open and interchangeable, so that your totem bird might be an owl, but your Bird of Night might be, for instance, a swift. Sometimes the Bird of Night remains within the conventional nocturnal category of species. Its purpose is to help your totem bird unlock doors in your psyche which can only be opened at night.

A simple way to discover the identity of your own Bird of Night and Bird of Day is as follows:

Breathe slowly, gently and quietly until you find the point of peace within. Begin to imagine you are standing in a sunlit glade, deep in the woods, in the first hour of the morning. The dawn chorus of the birds rises in a crescendo as you wait in peace beneath a brilliant blue sky touched with rose in the east. After a few moments, silence descends, as if the world has fallen still in anticipation. Stretch out your right arm. Say: 'I am…' followed by your name. Command your own Bird of Day to come to you, as if you were calling a loved friend. Wait patiently until your totem bird perches on your arm. Register clearly to which species it belongs.

As you continue to stand in the woodland glade, the sky darkens into black midnight, and the stars come out across the heavens in their bright myriads. The Moon shines full above the glade. Stand and listen to the hushed secret sounds of the night. Stretch out your left arm and say 'I am…' followed by your name. Command your own Bird of Night to come to you, again as if you were summoning a dear friend. Wait quietly until your totem bird appears on your arm. Discern its species.

It is important to note that in some rare cases, either bird might exhibit an amalgamation of different species, or even bear mythological characteristics. If this does happen, you will find that the summoned birds will always bear the marked features of one particular species. This is your totem bird. The characteristics with which the bird is endowed that relate to actual species indicate that these birds too have special significance for you, although this significance is shadowed. They relate to your actual totem bird in the way that your rising sign relates to your sun sign. They do not hold centre stage in the hierarchy of relevance relating to you, but their influences are nevertheless important.

However, I would like to sound a warning note respecting flights of fancy regarding this matter, as sometimes these can be spurious.

If your totem bird of either night or day truly manifests as a bird of mythology, it will do so without any influence of expectation or wish-fulfilment emanating from the lower mind, where desires and tendencies towards self-aggrandizement often take hold. If we are not careful to purify ourselves of such influences before performing the ceremony, we may find that our ego steps in and provides us with fabulous totem birds which are in fact only an aspect of our conceit! Generally, it is fair to say that in the use of this oracle we are aiming to embrace and penetrate the mystery of the spiritual essence of actual birds, which is a rich and splendid dimension indeed, and requires no fantastical elaboration!

Once you have discovered the identity of your totem Birds of Night and Day, you can call on them to help you read the bird oracle. First, call on your Bird of Day, and put your question to it. Ask it, as an extension of the ceremony given above, to summon to you a bird, perhaps more than one, that bears an appropriate message for you within the pages of the bird oracle. Wait patiently for the bird or birds to arrive and note down their species under the heading 'Day'. Now call on your Bird of Night, and repeat the procedure. Turn to the listings of the birds you have noted down within the oracle, and study their messages.

The birds summoned by your Bird of Day will provide you with positive, affirmative answers, linked with guidance on action and decision. Combine these answers with the entry given in the oracle for your Bird of Day. The birds summoned by your Bird of Night will highlight warnings, dangers, alternative paths, hidden aspects and underlying currents that might affect the outcome of the scenario concerning which you have sought counsel. Again, view these messages in the light of the oracle message given for your Bird of Night.

You can also ask your Birds of Day and Night to help you in similar vein according to their different perspectives. For instance, your question might be: 'Will this relationship develop into one that is lasting and worthwhile?' The bird selected by your Bird of Day will give you a clear, analytical, almost pragmatic answer, whereas that selected by your Bird of Night will offer you a more psychic and mystical overview related to the soul factors which are likely to come into play. The Bird of Night is particularly skilled in the art of throwing light on your dreams and your hidden motivations and aspirations. The Bird of Day will help you to identify and clearly delineate your aims and objectives, and indicate how these may best be achieved.

If ever your Bird of Day or your Bird of Night makes its presence felt in your psyche with particular keenness, simply refer to the entry in the oracle that concerns it. Even if you have read it on several previous occasions, it will still be worth studying again. Words in different circumstances and framed within different emotional perspectives and time frames bear different messages and meanings.

Because of the number of birds listed, it has not been possible to supply readers of this oracle with an accompanying set of cards. Nevertheless, if you have the patience, you can make your own set by marking down each bird specified within these pages on a separate piece of card, and then shuffling and drawing them as you would if you were using the tarot, or any other oracular card pack.

The methods listed above outline the traditional ways of using an oracle. However, by far the most powerful and instructive use of this oracle will arise from your own communion with birds as described in the previous chapter and the Introduction. Let those birds that have meaning for you as you live your life make themselves known to you. They will not fail to draw your attention to them, but it is essential to remain alert, present and responsive to their proximity, or you will miss the vital sign expressed by their manifestation and the guidance and encouragement they seek to bear to you. (You will no doubt find a comprehensive handbook on birds helpful in identifying the lesser-known species.)

When consulting the Oracle of the Birds, it is helpful to keep in mind that bird messengers and visitants are by no means restricted to those that may appear to you in their physical form, whether in your garden, whilst you are walking or driving, through your window or which seem significant to you as they fly across the skies. Birds can bring messages and teachings to you in dreams, in pictorial form, in the chance words of others. They can fly into your thoughts and linger long enough in that ever-changing landscape to leave you the gift of their message. They can even appear in stories which suddenly present themselves to be read

(Jonathan Livingstone Seagull, The Nightingale and the Rose, etc.). They might appear on a television advertisement or programme, in a magazine, or even in artwork and songs. When I was going through an extreme period in my life, the classical refrain 'Ah poor bird / Take thy flight / Up above the sorrows / Of this dark night' kept singing itself through my mind. I heeded the advice, and the bird became my rescuing angel.

If you are accustomed, in the mundane sense, to seeing a certain type of bird at some point in your everyday circuit, such birds will usually have no augural significance for you. This does not, of course, mean that when the time is appropriate, they cannot take on divinatory significance. It is a matter of sensitively judging how you might suddenly be alerted to a bird that you generally encounter on your daily round, of recognizing a new and evocative resonance in your experience of it. This will not necessarily happen within a dramatic setting or under exceptional circumstances – it is much more likely to be just a sudden flash of insight within a given moment. If this happens, then such a bird bears an augury for you. Here is a typical example: I have several birdfeeders hanging on a bush outside my study window, so I am accustomed to watching blue tits come and go all day. Because of this, I would not normally draw an augury from the appearance of such birds. Whilst taking a break one day recently and gazing out of the window, I began to think rather dolefully of a project that I had been attempting to move forward for more than a year, and of how it was probably impossible to expect good news after such continual frustration of my efforts. At that very moment, whilst the thought was still formulating, a blue tit (meaning happiness, a happy outcome, and the admonition to look at things in a different way) alighted on the sprig of a rosebush next to where the feeders hang, and gave a little trill. I immediately realized that this was an augury, and, sure enough, within a few days, confirmation came that at last things were progressing favourably.

As you draw closer to the birds and begin to feel a real kinship with them, you can put questions and appeals for help directly to them. Do this simply by speaking to them, either in meditation or (and perhaps preferably) by verbalizing your request in their presence, either out in nature or wherever they may congregate, or in your garden, or from an open window or doorway. Trust that the birds will, in a short time, send you a messenger from their prophetic clan.

Occasionally, within the context of the oracle, the bird augury will advise you to seek help from a specific bird. In this case, seek out a quiet spot either indoors or out, where you will not be disturbed. Hold a picture of the bird in your mind (you may well need a field-guide to do so) and call it three times by its species name. It is likely at this point to communicate to you its spirit name, which you may use from that point on. Ask your guardian angel to link your soul with the soul of the bird, and ask for the help that the augury specifies and that you have decided you would like to receive. Rest a little while in meditation. Nothing may come to you at this point. You may find yourself simply enjoying the soulful proximity of the bird you have called on, or just appreciating the silence and stillness. Ask your angel to enfold you in its wings, seal your crown, forehead, throat, heart and solar plexus centres with a cross of light within a ring of light, and gently emerge from your meditation. Within a short time, perhaps an hour, perhaps a day, perhaps a week, you will receive a response, and guidance will begin to flow to you as if from your own thoughts. It is as well to thank the bird and your angel after you have finished your inner communion.

Along with your own soul-perception (your most important learning tool) it is worthwhile to engage in further research the meanings of birds as they specifically relate to your own culture, either through mythology, folktale or fairy tale. Although no knowledge is ever set in stone, and such researches may not always be relevant to your personal bird encounters, it is as well to bear in mind the inheritance of meaning which has come down to us from ancient times, often bestowed, it seems, by spirits and angels themselves.

It is worth noting that the word 'auspice', meaning a portent, a prophecy or a prognostication, derives from a Latin word meaning 'an observer of birds'. Every culture recognized by recorded history has paid tribute to the spiritual potency of birds and their power of augury. From the earliest days of Imperial Rome, the College of Augurs was established as a sacred academy consulted by the emperors, who were guided implicitly in their policy-making by the observations and inter-pretations on their behalf by the collegiate diviners. It might be considered a prophecy in itself that, when it was finally disbanded in the 4th century AD, the complete dissolution of the Roman Empire followed soon afterwards. The academicians within the College of Augurs also studied omens from other sources, but their main concern was with those drawn from birds. Similarly, monks from many orders studied the flight formations and behaviour of birds, drawing lettering from the patterns they made in the sky.

Space has been provided at the end of this book for your personal notes and observations, and for recording your own growing relation-ship with the birds, so that when you put it to use you may draw on your own experiences within the oracle as a whole as well as the A–Z reference. This reference provides a key to the interpretation of the magical and revelatory Language of the Birds; yet it is your own heart-perception which will lift you into its greatest and most sublime wonders, and which will grant you familiarity, fluency and, ultimately, the joy of mastery.

The Oracle of the Birds

The spiritual secret of our delight in the joyousness of the lark's song, or in that of mavis or merle, is because the swift music is a rapture transcending human utterance.

Fiona Macleod

Albatross

The albatross is a bird of healing. Pipes carved from its beak were considered sacred talismans by sailors and many indigenous peoples of the South Sea Islands. This bird may certainly come to you over the airwaves via the medium of music! Its soul-message is one of peace, solace and freedom after many trials and sorrows. This great white bird is a symbol of the ascended soul, the Higher Self, and, naturally, to harm it or capture it symbolically brought misfortune to the perpetrator. It is one of the symbols of Christ-consciousness. When the majestic albatross comes to you, you are being asked to rise in spirit, in consciousness, to the higher spheres of beauty, healing and quietude.

In Britain, two angel birds in the shape of albatrosses are said to escort the soul of the Bishop of Salisbury into the spiritual worlds on his death. Many people through the centuries have seen these two supernatural birds, and there exist two well-documented cases in comparatively recent times: the first in 1885 before the death of Bishop Moberley, and the second in 1911, on the death of Bishop Wordsworth.

Aloysius Horn described the albatross as 'six feet of wafting snow'. Its great wings carry it in silent gliding motion high above the heaving waves, which we might interpret as a signature of our emotional and mental bodies. It appeared to him as a creature of dream and higher vision, a manifestation of serene tranquillity. This mode of still-winged and silent flight caused sailors to speak of it as sleeping on the wing, and indeed all the symbolism pertaining to this bird reveals it as a bird of meditation, urging us to take up this practice as a regular feature of our diurnal life for our blessing, healing and protection.

The albatross cries to you: 'Come to be comforted and healed and made new in the spiritual worlds, even whilst you live on Earth in a physical body; look at the bigger picture, and know that all darkness must pass, must transform into Light!'

Auk (Little)

The little auk is an intrepid seabird. It winters out in the open ocean, and is generally seen in Britain only when storm winds blow it ashore. With black-and-white plumage it flies with a rolling motion and whirring wing-beats. Its drumming rhythm sounds the imperative to advance, to push on through the storm.

Traditional wisdom respecting the little auk tells us that it comes into prominence in a prophetic sense to remind us that the tempests and rough weather in our lives will not leave us empty-handed, but rather will usher something worthwhile, even precious, into our sphere of being. We will feel a new co-ordination, a new felicity, spring to life within the structure of our soul, and consequently we will walk our path with greater dignity and strength of purpose, and a deeper joy than it was previously possible to contain. Except when it is nesting, the auk is silent, and, like the albatross, urges us to develop the habit of meditation so that we may better assimilate the gifts of the storms through which we pass.

The message of the little auk is: 'This stormy weather is about something that will eventually become clear to you. All is well. Roll with the punches, and remember that you are invincible!'

Avocet

This elegant black-and-white wader, with its delicate legs and ethereal beak, speaks to us of the intrepid nature of the soul. Although it is a bird suggestive of refinement and grace with marked agility in flight, it will fearlessly see off intruders, whatever their size.

When it spreads its wings, the markings across its back and wingspan are reminiscent of a shamanic ceremonial mask, telling us of its link with the Otherworld. It reminds us of the insistent voice of our soul or divine self. If we are refusing to pay heed to our inner voice, if we have strayed off course and consistently fail to adjust our behaviour or take the right path, the avocet comes calling, mirroring the urgency of the intuitive voice within ourselves.

It cries: 'Pay heed! You can end your suffering; you can avert calamity! Pay heed!'

Barnacle Goose (*see also* GOOSE)

These wild geese of marshland and seashore fly into our soul-sphere so that we may hear their keening cries and throw off the shackles of outworn conditions and all that keeps our soul in stasis. When the wild geese fly, be prepared to let your wild spirit fly with them and make changes in your life where routine, hesitancy or timidity may be stifling you and holding your true self in stultification. No wonder that those who wish to cling to obsolete structures and live life in a repetitious rut fear the cries of these birds and shiver when they see them, calling them birds of ill-omen!

There is an old belief that these birds were never hatched, but formed from restless driftwood on the high seas. Birds of the turbulent, ever-travelling, rootless wave, their wildness calls to our own wild nature and reminds us that we are not rooted in dull pettiness but are instilled with majesty and magnificence as the crashing breakers of the charging ocean.

Their message to us, like the fairy people in Yeats' poem, is: 'Come away, come away!'

Bee-Eater

This brightly plumaged bird with its balletic flight patterns is a symbol of joyousness in living, of zest for life. It seeks the heights, and congregates in the uppermost branches of trees or upon telegraph wires, where its wide aerial perspective grants it the best view for spying and seizing upon its insect prey.

It is a bird that aspects the summer of our years, the high life, the good times, the golden moments, the elevated points upon our route. Its spirit wisdom urges us to rejoice in life, and counsels us actively to seek out the inspiration to transform the plain water of our lives into wine. However, the bee-eater enshrines a simple but profound wisdom in its symbolism. When it swoops on bees and other stinging insects, it transports them to its lofty perch and carefully removes their sting before enjoying its meal, showing us how mindfulness will protect our well-being and happiness from the poisoned barbs which lurk within pleasure.

Its trilling, melodic message is: 'Let the good times roll, but first remove their sting!'

Bittern (*see also* HERON)

The eerie booming call of the bittern across the marshes has caused it to be associated with many strange legends of lost souls, lamenting apparitions and lonely, prophesying spirit voices. This bird carries the power of portent. It sounds a drum roll. If the bittern makes itself known to you, something hidden is about to emerge. This might bring joy or sorrow, perhaps even both.

The bittern is particularly associated with the sanctuary of the reed bed. The reed was one of the sacred 'trees' of the Druids, and was revered because its whispering voice murmured the secrets of the ages. The reed is a signature of our intuition, the 'still, small voice' within. We cannot hear the haunting boom of the bittern, either in actuality or in our imagination, without hearing too the gentle counselling wisdom of the reeds.

The bittern cries: 'Have no fear of what I herald, for you will be shown the path through the wilderness, and you will be guided faithfully every step of the way.'

Blackbird

The blackbird is the bird of the dreamtime, the magical worlds of unearthly beauty and enchantment within the consciousness of our soul. In Scotland's Western Isles it is called the merle, suggesting Merlin, the Prince of Enchanters himself. It stands at the sacred gateway between the two worlds of physicality and the spirit. It is linked with the twilight, the earthly symbol of this mysterious doorway.

It belongs to the thrush family, but in legend it is associated with the crow family. Of all the black birds, it is the one who can sing with the sweetness of Orpheus' lyre, and has a golden beak, signifying that it speaks and sings with the voice of the spirit. The Druids associated it with sweet joyousness, believing it bids us with its jubilant songs to have no fear of passing between the portals that link this world and the Otherworld that calls us with its magic and poetry. It is also the bird of the divine forges, telling us not to be afraid to take our soul into the smithy and allow life itself, He who is the goldsmith and She who is the smith of platinum and silver, to wreak their marvels and wonders upon our deepest being. If you hear the blackbird's call at a time when life for you seems appalling, is not this divine smithwork what is really happening to you? Melt in the fire, do not resist, and you will be transformed.

Listen to the song of the blackbird as twilight steals upon the world. It is the inner call of your soul, singing you into the enchanted worlds. Go deep within, and gather riches there. In ancient Europe, the blackbird was called the Black Druid, the bird of kindly spells and wisecraft. In Welsh myth, the miraculous birds of Rhiannon, who lulled the everyday mind to sleep and awakened the mystic soul, were blackbirds.

The magical Smith of the World, who, by divine commission, was given everything in creation as material to forge himself from, so the result of his angel-tended handiwork might reflect the exquisite magnificence of the perfect human image dwelling in glory in the eye of God, was accompanied in his sacred mission by a blackbird. The Smith represents humanity; he was a blacksmith, bringing gold forth from the sacred darkness, firing iron with the dispensation of light, for the blackbird is the bird of the sacred darkness.

The blackbird's haunting notes call: 'Live in the beauty and mystery of your soul! Be in the world, but not of it!'

Blackcap

This little bird of beautiful song shows us the meaning of the 'shining darkness' or the positive aspect of darkness. Intimations of its mystery are reflected in the poet Lord Byron's lines: 'She walks in beauty, like the night / Of cloudless climes and starry skies.'

The darkness bears a beautiful secret as the night bears the stars. If the darkness is oppressing you, think of the blackcap's song, one of the loveliest of all bird songs. There is treasure in the darkness as there are stars at night. Whilst the darkness seems to take things away, it also gives vision and brings dimension into being within us.

Sometimes, however, as it painfully creates its interior sculpture, it tempts us to fall prey to intolerance, harshness, condemnation of others, and to begin to shut down and deal in death where the heart and the emotions are concerned.

The blackcap warns against judgmentalism, towards ourselves as well as others, and against allowing death thoughts (thoughts of bitterness, despair, hopelessness and self-loathing) to crowd around us as we pass through darkness, because they only cause needless suffering and their counsel is always false.

The female actually wears a red cap, signifying the fires of the heart and the spirit which have the power to drive back the darkness.

The blackcap sings: 'Come into my cascade of song, and know that the heart is always free. The darkness and the light work together to create more life, more light, and every death-sentence is made null and void by the greater law of love!'

Bluebird

The bluebird denotes happiness. It is the sign of transcendent joy, of the spell of winter banished by the sweet days of spring. Very ancient mythology (pre-Celtic) tells that there is a paradise dwelling deep within us, a divine world which is the mother of all Edens, even of that recorded in the Bible which, in a golden age, was realized on Earth. The bluebird was said to have purposely escaped, as an act of divine mercy, from this primordial heaven into our world at the time when the Earth fell from grace and became as it is today, to remind us of what we have lost, and to inspire us to regain it. This idea of the bluebird flying into materiality from the inner sanctum of the heart is perhaps why it is so often associated with lovers and newborn babies.

It has been remarked that the idea of a blue bird signifying paradise and human happiness is strange, considering the idea of the historical 'blue devils' and the general concept of 'the blues'. In fact this idea arose from the fact that, in Elizabethan times, it was noticed that workers who used a certain type of indigo dye for colouring cloth became affected by depression and mental disturbances. The problem was discovered to lurk in the components of the dye, and the colour blue itself is therefore exonerated! Of course, mystics and occultists have always upheld blue as the colour of inner peace and mental repose, and there is no happier sight than a sky of clear blue.

The bluebird, by tradition part of this higher ether, sings and speaks similarly of unalloyed happiness.

Bluethroat

This robin-like bird bears a vivid blue throat. Its blue bib is encircled by narrow bands of black, white and chestnut with a centre spot of red or white. When this little bird comes into prominence in your life, it comes to highlight the important throat chakra or centre, which is located in the hollow of the throat. Strangely enough, seers report that the throat chakra glows violet-blue, transforming into a fiery or white gold at its mid-point. Its element is indeed the white ether, from which all form is brought into being and is also the mystical space in which it is contained. The throat chakra is associated with the goddess Brigid (Divine Daughter), whose name, although deriving from 'bright', is also a form of 'Brid' or 'Bird'. Beautifully carved birdhouses honouring this daughter-mother goddess were placed by her numerous devotees as altars and shrines for her blessing throughout many parts of the world in ancient times.

The throat chakra is linked with a soul difficulty known as 'enslavement to the body', wherein the demands of the physical and material life threaten to overwhelm spiritual sensitivity and wisdom. The throat chakra is also connected to our sense of hearing and listening, and with our ability to communicate. It is this gift of communication that the bluethroat underlines, telling us that an opportunity involving the art of communication has appeared or is about to appear, or perhaps that we may be failing to communicate effectively at an important junction in our lives.

The keyword for the throat chakra is 'silence', and the bluethroat teaches us that we must begin to honour the silence. We can do this best by learning to meditate, which will give peace and ensure that 'enslave-ment to the body' is gradually overcome. I am quite convinced that birds themselves do actually meditate, or, to be more accurate, are firmly attuned to the meditative rhythm of creation, in which the all-pervading breath of the indwelling Spirit is constantly drawn within, back to its ineffable source, and then given out as a divine act of creation.

Listening to the colonies of birds in my garden, I have noticed that, without fail, their songs and chirrups follow a pattern of prolonged bursts, followed by a moment or two of complete silence. After five or six seconds, a few birdcalls sound the signal that the rest period is over, and the chorus starts up again – only to die away entirely a little while later, and then to resume in the same vein. The rhythm is continuous and never-failing, so it seems as if there is some sort of communal meditation going on!

The message of the bluethroat is: 'Come into the sacred silence, and there find your daily rest and renewal!'

Blue Tit (and all the TIT family)

These charming little acrobats remind us to look at life from a different perspective. They delight in hanging upside down and turning head over heels in the bushes, exercising their viewpoint from all sorts of different angles! The great tit and the blue tit both have splashes of bright yellow plumage, which denotes the mind, as yellow is its colour. Their message is for us to prevent our minds from becoming set and rigid, always seeing everything from one narrow angle. The dainty titmouse family reminds us to be nimble, pliant and acrobatic in our thinking and views, to be graceful inhabiters of the airy regions, which are the mind's true element, and not to cling to Earth so that our minds become inflexible and tomb-like.

Yellow also suggests joy, and blue birds always bring happiness, so both these little titmice symbolize the delight of the soul when our mind allows its airs to blow freely and sweetly across the contours of its landscape.

They say: 'Your happiness is there in your soul; look at life in a different way and you will find it!'

Brambling

This bird is known as the 'northern chaffinch', and bears many similarities to its cousin. It also has the same power of augury (*see* CHAFFINCH *and* FINCH).

Bullfinch (*see* FINCH)

Bunting (*see also* FINCH)

The bunting family is associated with the Earth goddess. Whether they hop in and out among the corn or call from the reeds, they spend a lot of their time on the ground. They are mediators between heaven and Earth, and are especially linked with the spiritual task of subtle announcing or heralding. They flit in and out of our field of vision to tell us that something of import is about to happen, and that this event will have to do with completion or fulfilment.

From a humble, homely point of view, the cornucopia or the horn of plenty is associated with the bunting, and it generally announces or heralds something worth celebrating in a simple and homespun sense.

Their message is: 'Little blessings, little joys, little grains of golden corn, make up the bread of life!'

Buzzard

The buzzard's eyes are the same size as human eyes. When it mates, the male encircles the female high in the sky, constantly gazing straight into her eyes.

This bird symbolizes fearless honesty; honesty of soul, honesty and constancy of love. If you need courage to achieve this virtue, if you need to dispel the deviousness of others, or if you have yourself, perhaps unconsciously, been tempted into deviousness, this bird comes with a soul-teaching to rescue you.

Capercaillie

This enormous game bird with its displaying fantail resides mainly in pine forests. It has associations with Merlin, with the third eye or brow chakra, and with the sixth sense. Although it was more widespread prior to 1785 when it became extinct in Britain, it has remained confined to Scotland since its reintroduction in the 19th century. This is interesting, as Scotland is home to many families which pass down the gift of 'second sight' as a direct inheritance, and it is this faculty of second sight or 'sixth sense' which is the particular function of the third eye or the pineal gland.

The term 'pineal' derives from the word 'pine', because the gland itself looks like a miniature pine cone. No matter how old they grow, pine cones retain the ability to close under wet conditions and to open again when they are dry. This undying spark of soul-intelligence is in itself indicative of the action of the third eye, which, from a spiritual perspective, similarly opens and closes according to atmospheric conditions. When fully extended, the outer base of the pine cone forms a perfect representation of a chakra as it is viewed in the ethereal worlds, which is as a disc of petals containing the sacred spiral within its ring.

The capercaillie is linked with the Sun and the Moon through, respectively, its association with the forest pine which is a tree of the Sun, and its sacrificial aspect as nourishing food which connects it with the nurturing Mother Goddess whose symbol is the Moon. When we catch inner or outer sight of this reclusive bird, we are being asked to consider the magical aspect of life and our deeper purpose on Earth. The capercaillie foretells an opportunity to awaken our third eye or to increase its power, and advises us to be alert to this opportunity of awakening, for it will bring with it a certain wisdom or shamanic 'medicine' that we need at a particular stage in our lives.

The third eye is known esoterically as 'the Abode of Joy', and, in association with the opening of the third eye and all matters connected with inner vision, this bird prophesies the coming of joy into a life. This joy might even arrive explosively and give cause for celebration and carousal, as expressed by the capercaillie mating song which, with its components of double grinding or clicking ending in a prominent pop, sounds like the uncorking of a bottle of champagne!

Chaffinch

These delightful little birds can bring us knowledge from the heaven worlds. An old country saying advises 'Ask the finches' (*see* FINCH). Put your question to them and observe their behaviour!

The chaffinches are among the first heralds of spring, and their ancient habit was to approach the threshing floor or the area around the barn door and search for the golden grain amidst the chaff. The chaffinch bids us use the high tide of our life-energies in discerning the precious grain rather than chasing the empty illusory chaff.

Chiffchaff

This mercurial little bird, herald of the spring and its rising tides, bids us wisely foster and coordinate the high-octane energies that burn within us. These intense nervous energies encourage us to live life at the high-water mark, stimulating and firing our emotional, artistic and mental levels of being to their highest sensitivity. Yet their dynamics, if over-strained and overused, can actually cause blockages and scrambling in the very arenas of the psyche to which they at first lent such inspiration.

The active, flitting, intense and restive little chiffchaff, whose name sounds like a small frenetic engine, seeks solitude and the cool depths of the woods to balance its high-paced nature. We can do the same, enjoying the sanctuary of nature and of the calming, centring practice of meditation. Little 30-second breaks spent breathing gently and quietly, in contemplation of some tranquil object or symbol, help to restore the equanimity of human chiffchaffs!

Chough

The chough is similar in appearance to the jackdaw, although the chough is entirely black except for its red feet and bill. It inhabits rocky coasts and mountain crags, where it takes spectacular flight around lonely peaks and imposing rock-faces. Its association with majestic heights and the rolling sea, with the west of the British Isles, and with the black bird's timeless connection to the hidden worlds of mystery and wonders, links it with Arthur, the mariner king and warrior who held the supreme seat of majesty in the land during his 40-year reign, known as the Peace of Arthur. The last breeding pair in England had their residence in Cornwall in 1952, the place of King Arthur's birth. Its decline surely cannot be due to nest-robbing or hunting, because a curse was said to descend on anyone who stole eggs from its nest or harmed the bird in any way due to the belief that the soul of King Arthur lived on in the chough. The raven shares the same legend, although some believe it was King Arthur's first queen, his true consort, whose spirit is magically enshrined within this impressive bird.

The evocative call of the chough, with its keening lament, reminds us of the legend that Arthur will return with his queen to lead their people to freedom and joy in the new age, which is associated with our own time.

When the chough draws near to those seeking augury, it communicates to the diviner that the truth, nobility and strength of Arthur is at their back and at their helm, and that their mission is blessed and accompanied by his warrior's heart in its royal compass of courage, justice and mercy.

Cock

The cock is a sun-bird and signifies the Martian energies. He is a bird of many beautiful myths and fables. He drives away the encroaching world of shadows and its dim, sinister intelligences and affirms the magic of the dawn and the morning. He often crows throughout the night as watchful protector. He alerts us to the presence of spirits, and announces the coming of a stranger. The cock also symbolizes purity and can detect impure motives. The greatest momentous events regarding the human soul are marked by his plumaged voice.

A story documented in Aubrey's *Remaines* relates how when a man called Ashton was leaving his home to travel to France, the cock crowed on the instant that he stepped out of the house with such striking synchronicity that his wife took a message of warning from it, and was troubled, afraid that he would never set foot on his own threshold again. Sure enough, the poor man was arrested at sea, tried and executed. This is one of many hundreds of similar tales which attest to the cock's divine ability to announce a warning.

His crow, given forth many times with unusual volume at a time of day when he is generally quiet, foretells a pregnancy. In Lincolnshire, it was the tradition that the first pancake to be made on Shrove Tuesday must be given to the cock, and that no further cake could be produced until he had received it. The number of hens which rushed to help him eat it predicted the number of years that the daughter of the house would have to wait before she married.

His cry marks the profound moments on the clock face of ultimate human destiny. A spirit cock called when the world began, and has subsequently called at the birth of every great teacher or hero, particularly at the birth of Christ. It also marked the disciple Peter's treachery against the Christ, an act which, according to new evidence, had far greater repercussions on the fate of humanity than has previously been understood. A Christian tradition also states that the cock's crow will initiate the Last Day. Similarly, the Vikings believed that the dawn of Ragnnarock, the day upon which all living things were destined to meet their doom, would be pronounced by the crowing of a gold-crested cock.

White cocks are lucky, and harbour magical powers. They are believed to protect the household to which they belong. A story from Fife tells how a group of sailors twice saw, from a ship lying off the coast, a meteor falling towards a farmer's haystacks, but on each occasion a white cock crowed before it struck, and the meteor instantly changed course and landed where it did no harm. The sailors were so impressed that they persuaded the farmer to sell them the miraculous bird. The night following the purchase, a third meteor fell in the rick yard and set all the ricks alight.

The black cock was said to carry remarkable healing powers, and facilitated magical workings. The cock's first vocal salute of the day is said to be a rite of purification against the dark. His stentorian cry bids us: 'Behold the glory of the dawn and the morning which belong to the Sun! Feel this golden energy, which is also consciousness, ever coursing through your heart and remember that you are rooted in it!' The cock's crow also warns us to be on guard against people, psychic forces, or our own hidden dark side which would waylay us.

Coot

The augury of the coot is similar to that of the moorhen (*see entry*). The difference is that there is an element of humour to the coot's message. It reminds us of the hilarity in the ridiculousness of life's trials, and prognosticates that humour, a light touch and light spirits will serve us best in the situations or conflicts we are seeking to resolve when it presents itself through divination.

Cormorant

This fisher bird has sometimes been called an underwater falcon, because it can hunt shoals deep under the waves with consummate skill. It is a bird of storms and lightning, of shipwreck and sorrow, known as the 'parson' in some districts because of its sombre plumage. It reminds us of the sweetness of sorrow, and of how this visiting spirit can bring healing and nourishment to our deepest self. It bids the angels of sorrow to gently surround us with their magic and keening beauty, knowing that sorrow brings its own awakening and its own comfort.

Charles Swainson reported an incident in 1860 where a cormorant alighted on the steeple of Boston Church in Lincolnshire and sat there until the following day, refusing to move until eventually the sexton shot the unfortunate creature. The visitation of the cormorant was spoken of throughout the town as a serious omen of ill-boding, and many people wondered fearfully what grave news would follow the appearance of the 'old man of sorrow.' Sure enough, news arrived of a catastrophe very soon afterwards – the sinking of the ship *Lady Elgin* and the loss of her 300 passengers.

The cormorant feeds plentifully, pointing to the rich spoils of learning and soul-nutriment which come to the human spirit when the storms of life rage, when we feel the blast of the lightning and the shipwreck of our hopes.

The cormorant cries: 'Let the Great Deep swallow your shipwrecks and move on, knowing you are free from all ties and burdens. Don't hold on to the bad energy of regret, resentment or disappointment. All is well! All is well!'

Corncrake

The corncrake calls through summer's prime and is a deeply secretive bird, rarely seen, although its hoarse, croaking rasp is unmistakable. John Clare calls it a 'fairy bird'. Once inhabiting the woodlands, it is now a bird of grain and grass, living among the golden corn. The corncrake reminds us that, although the many secrets of life and the soul cannot be clearly seen from an everyday perspective, their resonances can be very clearly heard, and so discovered, if the student of the Language of the Birds will only listen with heart-centred attention and devotion to the Spirit of Life calling through all its mundane exteriors.

The call of the corncrake is strange and gruff, but magical; perhaps demonstrating to us that we should not only pay heed to conventionally pleasant sounds or situations, as others may have a beautiful message for us as well.

Crake (Spotted)

The spotted crake gives the same augury as the moorhen (*see entry*), with the difference that the spotted crake foretells that you will be required to make a series of little decisions, little choices. Despite their smallness, the outcome of these decisions will not be trivial.

This little water bird bids you take note of the water within, the inner pools of reflection and contemplation, which become still and clear when you allow yourself a period of quiet time and mindfulness to study their depths.

Crane (*see* HERON)

Crossbill (*see* FINCH)

Crossbill (Scottish) (*see* FINCH)

Crow (*see also* RAVEN)

The crow represents a more comical version of his more serious brother, the raven. Wisdom is his message, but he symbolizes its more amusing side, and especially our hilarious attempts to seek it and follow it.

His message is: 'Seek wisdom with a sincere but light heart, and don't be afraid to play the fool to express it or attain it!' He also comes to warn us that we are making ourselves ridiculous in a negative way through bitterness, despair or anger – in which case he invites us to laugh at him and ourselves, and be released.

Cuckoo

The cuckoo is a Goddess bird. The Old Woman of the Cuckoos, famous in the folklore of northern Europe, is Mother Earth herself, releasing numerous cuckoos in the springtime if she is pleased with humankind, and a paucity of the birds if she is not. The Estonians call her *Sinlinda*, the bird of summer. The Sanskrit villagers of ancient times hailed her as a divine messenger, *Kakila*, the bird who knows all things past, present and to be. These villagers would listen in awe as they heard her sing in the Himalayan solitudes.

The cuckoo is a bird of many legends; and all the old tales speak of her as a deity or as the Goddess, or as the spirit of enchantment. She brings the spring and heralds the summer. Her sweet voice, the 'bell of heaven', troubles the soul with longing. It is the voice of promise, the promise of Eden, of perfect, undiminishing erotic love, of worlds of joy and delight half-perceived by the awakened spirit; promises which cannot be fulfilled upon this Earth, but which our innermost self knows will be made good...in some far-off time, in some unearthly place.

The cuckoo promises Paradise, and all around us, when she calls, the green world breaks into blossom; there is fragrance and sunshine and the songs of nature. The cuckoo bids us absorb the loveliness of spring into our hearts, to cherish its presence and its promise throughout the year. She is the bird of promise, symbolical of the Earth Spirit's free-handed and open-hearted giving. Even her habit of laying her eggs one at a time in other birds' nests, which some people interpret as a negative trait, is indicative of this spirit of giving, even though she removes one of her host's eggs, holds it in her bill whilst replacing it with her own, then flies off and (ceremonially, according to Druidic wisdom) swallows it.

A true story concerning the cuckoo tells how one freezing, stormy night in April when the snow was falling thickly, a certain Farmer Moffatt and his wife of Towdenack in Cornwall welcomed a number of guests to their home for supper. Several of the guests commented on the dreariness and unseasonable extremity of the weather, voicing their fear that the true spring would not properly arrive in that year. Mrs Moffatt, who was rumoured to have descended from a line of wise women, suggested that they toast the Old Woman of the Cuckoos, said in legend to be the mother of all things, and petition her to change the weather. Farmer Moffat brought forth his finest port and filled their glasses as an appropriate salute to the occasion, and the company raised them in honour of the Great Mother, supplicating her to bring the spring. The fire leapt up as if in answer, and the farmer seized the biggest log on his hearth and cast it into the flames, as if half-seriously making an offering to the deity whom they had just toasted. To their loudly exclaimed astonishment, out from the hollow log flew a cuckoo, fluttering around the room and warbling its soft piping notes without apparently taking alarm. Mrs Moffatt let it out of the window and discreetly muttered her thanks to the spirit world. The next day dawned warm, bright and calm, and from then on it was 'a paradise of a spring, the best ever', according to locals.

The reverence of country people for the cuckoo as a Goddess bird (the fact that it is actually the male of the species that calls 'cuckoo', and that the female has a cascading, bubbling song which sounds quite different, was considered a mere detail, for the religious belief of the old faith was that the entire entity of the cuckoo was attuned to the Goddess) is evident in an old folksong:

> O the cuckoo is a pretty bird
> She sings as she flies;
> She bringeth good tiding,
> She telleth no lies;
> She sucketh white flowers
> For to keep her voice clear;
> And when she singeth 'cuckoo',
> Summertime draweth near.

It is customary to turn money over in your pocket and to make a wish when you first hear her soft fluting, as if from the fairy world, for your money will be increased and your wish fulfilled. The cuckoo is said to turn into a hawk during the winter, which is a reference to that aspect of the Goddess known as the crone, the wise woman who reveals the mirror of illusion so that we may recognize and know the essence of spiritual reality; therefore we experience the bitterness of winter, of painful scarcity, of cold and death, of predatory instinct rather than the divinely present heart and hands of abundant giving.

Everything that the cuckoo is in the spring is reversed in the winter. The idea that she becomes a hawk arises from magical perception, but it also partly derives from the harsh, laughing call of the male, the 'opposite' of his 'cuckoo', which is annunciated as 'gwork-gwork-gwork' or 'gowk-gowk-gowk', and from the fact that the cuckoo actually does resemble a small bird of prey. The winter hawk that the cuckoo transforms into is known in many areas as 'the gowk', and is said to bring storms in its wake. This harsh, mockingly laughing hawk and its ominous storms, although it exists only in concept, is indeed the mirror opposite of the benevolent, enchanted cuckoo. She is the mysterious wandering breath of the Divine.

Her message is: 'The eternal springtime, so transient in your world, is the true reality beyond the veil; remember this in the depths of winter, of your soul as well as that of the seasons. And remember too, that every one of your heart's desires will be brought to fruition, as the springtime promises; for this is the Law.'

Curlew

The lamenting, human cry of the curlew bears a Janus-faced message. This bird of wild moorland and lonely fell reminds us with its plaintive call that we must find our way back to our spiritual home whilst still on Earth, or we will indeed become lost souls, perhaps on the other side of the veil as well as on this.

Its second message tells us of the sorrow and the seduction of earthly illusion, including death and misfortune, and that all is not as it seems. Those who die are not dead; those who are ruined are not bereft, whilst the living and the fortunate may be both dead and ruined according to the judgment of the world of truth dwelling in the soul.

As in the vision of Francis Thompson, the poet, the curlews tell of the hound of heaven and the hound of earthly shadow. Whose quarry would you be? In northern Britain, the curlews are known as the Wisht Hounds, and in the south they are spoken of as Gabrel Hounds, those of the Wild Hunt.

The curlew cries of suffering and loss, but teaches us also of the safe and sure road out of these illusory pitfalls. Its message is: 'Pierce your heart to find life's key!'

Dipper

This little bobbing songster haunts rivers, streams and lakes, wandering into the water and walking beneath it at its margins to gather food. It inhabits two worlds, and its message concerns our choices between action and repose. There is a time to speak and a time to be silent, a time to act and a time to do nothing, a time to initiate and a time to let go.

The nodding dipper, with its sweet poignant song, affirms that it is right to do nothing until you are absolutely certain in the quiet depths of your soul that it is the time to act.

Diver (Black-Throated)
(N. America: Black-Throated Loon, Speckled Loon, Lesser Imber)

This water bird emphasizes commitment. When a potential project, a cause, a relationship, a new line of work or study, or perhaps the undertaking of a new skill or art presents itself to us, the diver bids us take a while to ponder the situation and to check for hidden resistance or unseen snags.

If the pointer in the heart does not falter, then, this bird tells us, dive in and give it your best!

Diver (Great Northern)
(N. America: Common Loon)

This larger diver gives the same augury as the black-throated diver, with an added emphasis on encouragement and reassurance. If you do decide to commit, this bird assures you that you certainly possess the vision, drive, energy, determination and the soul-attuned sensitivity to make a go of it.

Diver (Red-Throated)
(N. America: Red-Throated Loon)

The red-throated diver speaks to us of commitment after a period of wise reflection, as do the other divers, but in the case of this bird the augural note may also be taken up by the dipper (*see above*). The nuance in its message is that, although we must be certain before we decide to move forward (the dipper's wisdom), we must also realize that there is a time for everything under the Sun.

When the season is right, when the time is favourable, then we must seize the moment without timidity or hesitation.

Dodo

Surprisingly enough, this bird has presented itself as eager to participate in the *Oracle of the Birds*. It is extinct, as is commonly known. It belonged to the pigeon family, and was as big as a swan, although it was flightless as its wings gradually became too small to support its rotund body.

A scientifically accurate and pleasing portrait of the dodo exists in Tenniel's illustrations to Lewis Carroll's *Alice's Adventures in Wonderland*. The artist studied the dodo skeleton that was then on display in the British Museum, together with the representation accompanying it, which was an amalgam of ornithological knowledge based on the skeletal remains and early reports and sketches of the actual bird. Its main habitat was the island of Mauritius, where it was hunted out of existence by the middle of the 17th century, partly because of its trusting disposition. This sad and telling fate is part of its augury.

However, the latter is not quite what we may think. It is true that the dodo comes to us to issue a warning: predatory, self-interested people or organizations seek to take advantage of the good-willed, unsuspecting, trusting elements in our nature. Although it is necessary for us to 'wise up' about this, the dodo wishes us to consider its sacrifice. It was a bird of Goddess, of the Great Mother, of the free-handed, free-hearted play of forces we call Mother Nature.

The dodo's spiritual signature was nourishment, friendliness, open-heartedness, the embrace and nurture of strangers. Naiveté, over-optimism and an unawareness of danger must all be corrected, of course. A doormat mentality is certainly not what the dodo advocates. Yet it warns against the streetwise, aggressively self-protective attitude which sees cynical self-interest as the highest intelligence and strength, and which despises the gentle, meek and non-retaliatory.

The dodo's dove-like call cries: 'Protect yourself; do not bare your breast for the dagger; but remember that the principles of kindness, generosity, gentleness, and the refusal to put self-preservation first at all costs, are the true values. These principles will remain forever, even though I am no more!'

Dotterel

This northern-loving mountain bird is associated with the mighty goddesses and stone giantesses of the northern mountains and the polar stars. It carries the sacred fire at its heart, being warm-breasted in appearance. Folklore called old men 'dotterels' because the bird suggested a 'doting' tendency.

The dotterel is said to be so fond of imitation and so easily cajoled that anyone who excites its curiosity by strange antics may catch it. However, this is one of its 'reverse mimicry' characteristics, where it acts out for us in imitation the human soul's inclination to be led by the nose in its blind continuation of mindless habits imposed by custom and culture. Its teaching enshrines an opposite directive. Although it seems a silent, meek bird, trusting of humans, it is a symbol of feminine fire, of feminine power. It is a priestess among birds, leading us in spirit to the mountain tops, to vistas so limitless that they are cosmic in their sweep.

The dotterel reminds us that we need not allow domestic concerns to oppress, choke or limit us and that the femininity in man, in the human race, is a magnificent power, an imperishable fire, that we do not yet understand either biologically or spiritually.

The dotterel bids us bathe, to lustrate, in this fire and to relinquish to it all dross, all conditioning which seeks to make us less than we are.

Dove (including PIGEON)

These beautiful birds are the attendants of Divine Mother. They symbolize peace, and many psychics and seers have remarked on the fact that, when prayers are given for peace and healing, visionary flocks of these white messengers of the Goddess fill the skies or settle like a benediction on the landscape. Doves are sacred to Astarte, Aphrodite, Venus, Ishtar and the great Celtic goddess Brigid. They are also associated with the three spinning sisters (Past, Present and Future) who create our fate from combining the threads of our soul with the elements, with time, and with the three dimensions to make a body and a life-path for each of us.

White doves predict a wedding. In Christian symbolism, they are emblems of the Holy Spirit, the mother aspect of the Trinity. It is said that although vengeful spirits can transform themselves into any bird or animal shape, they cannot assume the image of a dove.

Pigeons, close cousins of the dove, share with them the angelic attribute of carrying the soul home upon its death, and there are, indeed, many reported (and well-authenticated) incidents throughout folk history of pigeons and doves seeming to perform this service. The birds arrive a few days before the death, and disappear a few days afterwards; they seem to assume guardianship over certain households or homesteads. The widespread superstition that a person cannot die whilst lying on a pillow in which there are doves' or pigeons' feathers, would seem to attest to the birds' spiritual teaching that there is no death.

Pigeons are earthly as well as heavenly messengers, and denote communication, the need for ordinary human communication and the need for this to progress into simple soul-to-soul communion. They feed their young on 'crop-milk', a sweet substance similar to mammals' milk. In one sense, they embody a vital link between the bird species, that of the mammalian human, and God the Mother.

The dove is a symbol of how, through attuning to the point of consciousness in the heart, we can give forth the Light in our spirit to heal, bless and bring peace to any situation or member of humanity, no matter how far distant they may be.

The dove sings: 'Breathe in the Holy Breath! Breathe out the radiance of your spirit! Transforming earthly conditions is your gift! Give it, give it, give it!'

Duck

The duck speaks to us of purified emotion. It is this sanctified emotion that the nature spirits express in their revels and in their life-mission, and, upon a yet more hallowed plane, that which moves the angels. An Islamic text, 'The Book of Mohammed's Ladder', states that Mohammed was borne on his visionary flight 'athwart the back of a duck'.

Purified emotion at its most sublime is the perfect vehicle for the manifestation of love, which is not in itself an emotion, but the power and source of spirit. The duck's strange, comical, laughing cry echoes the harshness of earthly experience, but proclaims that its greater purpose is to be transmuted into the power of love, and that an essential part of this transmutation is to absorb the blows and stumbles of earthly life into the alchemical process of humour. Then emotion has a safe earthly base, and a pure spiritual destination for its epic flights and voyages of discovery.

If we are approaching a situation in our life where great emotion is likely to come into play, the duck reminds us of these two containment points – the one at the earthly or most mundane level, which is copper-bottomed if it readily transposes distressed emotion into humour, and the other at the height of our aspiration, which, if it is love, will stand as surety against our getting lost in dark byways. Emotion in right relationship to the music of the soul is beautiful, the surging power of the Godhead and the god in humanity, but it becomes dangerous and destructive and ultimately without substance if it is not contained within these two points. That is why spiritual masters tell us that emotionalism (emotion indulged in purely for its own sake) destroys love.

The duck cries: 'Purify your emotional forces with love, and you will hit the mark every time!'

Dunlin

The dunlin is a spirit bird. Its haunt is wet moorland and salt marsh, and its mission is to bring earthly presence attuned to the spirit to lonely, desolate places, so that their incumbent spirits can be given a mode of expression that the physical world can see and understand according to the measure of percipience belonging to individual witnesses.

If the dunlin presents itself to you, something within yourself, within your environment or within your remit, that has so far been silent and undecipherable, is to be given presence, given voice. The dunlin is particularly fond of the Scottish isles, symbolic of those enchanted isles of the west where all noble desires of the heart are granted the grace of fulfilment.

Listen to this spirit bird; mark what it imparts to you. When you give expression to what has heretofore dwelt in the silence of the spirit, you will be given a new power, a new emancipation; but with this power comes responsibility, a need for mindfulness, and a duty to speak what is true.

Dunnock

This shy little garden bird harbours a profound and beautiful secret. It is the bird selected most often by the cuckoo to receive her egg into its nest. In one sense, this is unfortunate for the dunnock, because its nestlings pay the price of playing host to their planted sibling – they are squeezed out of their nursery due to the cuckoo chick's much greater size, and fall to their death. And yet in an esoteric sense the dunnock is in truth deeply honoured by the cuckoo's selection. Although because of it a sorrowful sacrifice is inevitable, the dunnock is nevertheless the chosen one, the beloved one, according to magical tradition. It is placed with as great a reverence on the altar of spiritual promise as that other sacred bird which it resembles – the sacrificial wren, beloved of the Druids and said by them to contain the knowledge of all things in its tiny precious egg. Wrens in particular are moved to assist the dunnock, or other host birds, to feed the single cuckoo chick within the ransacked nest.

If the dunnock makes itself known to you, it may come either before, during, or after a time of sorrow. The dunnock bids you dry your tears, because it bears to you the message of its twin soul, the cuckoo, who is the enchanted summer-herald. In spiritual interpretation, and in Fiona Macleod's words: 'Welcome that hour when the voice of the cuckoo floats through ancient woods rejoicing in their green youth, that voice which has in it the magic of all springs, the eternal cry of the renewal of delight.' Despite the presence of sorrow, know that your summer is coming. As an old folksong says in its refrain: 'When you hear the cuckoo, summertime draweth near.'

It is of that spiritual summer of the soul's delight that the dunnock tells, and when it brings its presence to your attention, you have caught the first whisper of the sweetness of that stealing breath as its incense of promise advances towards you.

Eagle

The magnificent eagle, symbol of St John in the Christian tradition, is said to be the emblem of the New Age, the Golden Age which we will enter when the terrible Age of Kali, the dark goddess of enlightenment-through-tribulation, has passed away into the brooding west. The golden eagle, bird of the Sun and messenger of the spirit, will bring in the Golden Age when we have truly learned the depth and glory of its symbolism. In recent history, as well as on numerous occasions throughout the ages, humanity made a baleful mistake in understanding the spiritual forces which the eagle represents, for this bird is the sigil for majesty, mastery and kingship; the power of empire, of legions, of hosts, of unimpeded progress, victory, splendour and strength.

The true understanding is perhaps that we should willingly and individually enter into the dominion of the Sun, behind which shines the ineffable Spiritual Light, so that all these glories may be added unto us for our illumined souls to conquer the dark forces of war, rapacity and oppression which arise from within ourselves. When we fail to understand, the very opposite happens. That is why, above the portals of the ancient mystery schools, the sign of the sun-eagle with outspread wings exhorted the entering student to 'Know Thyself.'

When we have attuned in full measure to this messenger from the pinnacle of the spiritual worlds, we will see the eagle's symbolical nature in its true light, and realize that as well as the positive aspects of the qualities already mentioned, the eagle signifies aspiration, ascension, inspiration, fruitfulness, faith, devotion, freedom, liberation of energy, celerity, keenness of vision, generosity, wisdom, mercy and immortality – all the facets of being which in truth comprise the perfected soul.

To the ancients, who held it in awe, it carried the supreme power of the god Jupiter, who was accompanied by an eagle. The eagle is often portrayed with a hare or a serpent in its talons, a sign of divine wisdom fallen to Earth (humanity entrapped in matter, with its divine aspects grounded) which the eagle will rescue and bear once again to the heavens. It was said of the eagle that it could gaze undazzled into the solar glory, and that it held this distinction of its blood in such high esteem that if one of its brood failed to express the divine inheritance, the mother threw the unfortunate eaglet out of the nest to expire. The symbol of the two-headed eagle represented the conjoining of the Holy Roman Empire; the German eagle faced toward the viewer's left (designated 'sinister' in heraldry), the Roman towards the right ('dexter').

We can see from a historical perspective how the mighty spiritual forces that the eagle commands were used by the Romans from the point of view of the spiritual masculine principle to conquer and rule, and from the standpoint or power-source of the feminine principle by the Nazis in an attempt to overpower human consciousness itself. Both are terrible distortions of the true spiritual heritage of humanity, which are its God-powers.

We need the eagle within us to gaze straight ahead, directly into the solar glory, and to dispel from the nest of our being any deviant eaglets that insist on looking to the right or to the left! Interestingly, considering the idea of the Holy Spirit or the Holy Breath, which are almost synonymous, the eagle in Norse legend is the spirit of the wind, the form in which Odin, the supreme deity, flew with song mead to the realm of the gods. Here he took his place at the head of the Cosmic Tree – Yggdrasil, the sacred ash tree. The eagle renewed its youth by flying so close to the Sun that its plumage caught fire, and then plunged into a secret lake to extinguish the flames. As its feathers grew again, so its youth was restored. This legend points to the wisdom of the eagle, for when the masculine solar force becomes dangerous and destructive, it plummets straight into its feminine hidden lake (in some tales it is the sea). It balances the masculine and feminine spiritual principles in perfect harmony, and thus expresses immortality, for this secret is the elixir of life.

To the student of the Language of the Birds, it brings the pure airs of exalted consciousness, the assurance of eternal renewal, and a bracing note of courage. It says: 'I am your ally on the Eternal Path. The attainment of soul-perfection is your birthright!'

Egret (Little) (see also HERON)

This elegant white heron bears the same message as the grey heron, only its promise tells of purification and fulfillment on a more intense scale. The grey heron bears an element of Saturnian philosophy, of the light penetrating the darkness. The white heron speaks of the dazzling sun-centre of our being, the heart and the shining brow. It speaks of the Bright Knowledge, and of spiritual achievement and healing beyond time and space.

The little egret calls: 'The fruition of all your striving is at hand, for your season has come!'

Eider

This plump sea duck, the size of a small goose, bears the same general message as the duck (see entry), with the particular addition that the eider speaks to us of our dream-life. Its feathers have been used to fill pillows and quilts for many generations, and its spirit has penetrated our deepest slumbering dreams. It reminds us that our emotions are most clearly revealed in our dream life.

If the eider duck makes itself known to us, we are ready to receive a message from our dreams. It will generally concern our emotional well-being, and perhaps the need for release and reconciliation. Do not be misled by the somewhat prosaic appearance of this particular duck. It is a gifted dream-guardian and is well-acquainted with the medicine of dreams.

Keep a notebook and pen by your bed, and upon waking write down whatever you can remember of your dreams, even if they are only snatches and fragments. A pattern and a story will soon begin to emerge. To explore these further, concentrate on capturing the feeling-tone of your most important dreams, and write a short story by entering fully into that feeling-tone with your creativity and imagination. Give the shrewd little eider duck a role in your tale.

Another helpful method of reworking your dreams is to set up a written dialogue with a leading dream-character, asking it important questions as to its significance and what it is trying to convey to you. If your dream-character does not respond easily, summon the eider duck and let it mediate between you, so that you ask your questions through its agency. It sounds like a strange technique, but it often works very well!

Eider (King)

The king eider carries the same general augury as the duck and the eider (*see individual entries above*), but it comes to impart one clear and simple message – a significant dream is imminent, and it is important that you should take note of it.

Fieldfare

A bird of the autumn and winter fields, the fieldfare arrives in August and leaves the shores of Britain in May. It is known by traditional romantic names such as the snow bird, the storm bird or storm cock. Its chattering song sings of the delights of winter and the autumn storms. Fieldfares gather in trees and face the wind.

In their winter wanderings, they seem to be the spirit of the frosty fields, reminding us that it is the breath of the spirit across the land which gives it its essence, its reality. The drowsy summer field is not the same as the field under autumn rains and suspiring mists, nor is there any resemblance between the field of vernal green busy with genial springtime activity and the field of winter whose frozen hollows are solid as rock and whose barren ridges bare a snow-white breast to the iron sky. The fieldfare is present in every season of the year, but it brings a special warmth, vitality and cheer to those months which might seem the least promising.

It bids us take delight in and eagerly explore that field of activity which the moment gives to us, whatever it is, and seek out its wonders and treasures however humble these gifts may appear. The sighing of the autumn winds and the unbosoming of the winter rains across the land can speak to us of beauty and mystery as well as dancing spring breezes and soft summer twilights.

Finch *(see also* BUNTING)

Heralds of spring and new beginnings, finches flock together with buntings and, occasionally, other small birds to create an impressive airborne tool of augury. An old country saying bids us 'Ask the finches' when we require an answer via divination. Watch the action of the flock:

- If they fly towards you whilst you hold your question in mind, or as their first action afterwards, the answer is yes.

- If they fly away, the answer is no.

- If the flock rises and falls, the answer is that your wish will be fulfilled after a few – or many, according to the behaviour of the flock – 'ups and downs'.

- If they land on the ground, they tell you that you will gain what you seek, perhaps after an initial disappointment or after the involvement of hard work in 'grounding' your purpose.

- If they land mainly in the trees and bushes, many little hopes will come to fruition, which will grant you strength to pursue your greater dream.

- A loud, clamorous flock indicates a busy, eventful time ahead.
- A quieter flock indicates a time of calm progress.
- An entirely silent flock (a rarity) sounds a warning.

However, whatever might befall us and whatever life throws at us, the finches always bring a message of hope and blessing, and a promise that all will be well in the end.

Their rich trilling songs proclaim: 'Hope is never lost or vain, because hope will reveal the sweet secret of life, whatever its pain! Keep a green bough in your heart and the singing bird will come!'

For easy reference, a list of portents identified by individual finches is given below:

Brambling (the 'northern chaffinch'): as CHAFFINCH below.

Bullfinch: the bullfinch reveals to us the sacrificial aspect of fire; we must give something in order to complete an initiation or cycle. The bullfinch sings: 'Sacrifice, and be blessed!'

Chaffinch (*see also individual entry*): the need for discernment is highlighted. Choose wisely, and beware the lure of pipedreams and wild-goose chases.

Common Redpoll: this bird, a little larger than the lesser redpoll, bears the same augural meaning, with the addition of an emphasis on clear delineation. The fire in your nature – your will, your enthusiasm, your sustained energy, your keen unwavering focus – will allow you to manifest those things to which you aspire in life. This larger redpoll cries: 'Wise use of this fire will bring you rich blessings; employ it to burn away the inessentials in your focus and to concentrate with unwavering inner gaze on your goals.' It tells us that this act of mind-cleansing is a vital facilitation of our inner fires; clear mental delineation of the potential we seek to make manifest is crucial to the process.

Crossbill: whilst the redpolls particularly love both pine and birch (the trees of, respectively, the masculine and the feminine inner fires), the crossbill, vividly red, cleaves solely to the pine forests, to the solar fire. Its message is very similar to that of the redpolls, except that it aspects the masculine force, and tells us to seek outward, decisive action in the physical world.

Goldfinch: the goldfinch is a bird of blessing. It speaks of inner, intuitive wisdom, the precious gold which is present in the blood, in the DNA of every human being, and which bears the stamp and impress of the soul's individuality, its own 'way home'. If others are putting undue pressure on you to follow their way instead of your own, the goldfinch encourages you to firmly take your power back and readjust your life according to your own soul-wisdom, your true source of gold. Thereby, your inflow of blessings from the universe will free itself from its inhibiters.

Greenfinch: the greenfinch is a fairy bird, and its presence denotes magic, mystery, inner journeying, and a time to read the signs of the universe to help us to an important interior realization and revelation. When you see the greenfinch, make use of poetry, sublime music, myth and fairytale, artistic endeavour, contemplation and meditation to open your imagination to higher vision and understanding. The greenfinch denotes a spiritual secret ready for revelation.

Hawfinch: the hawfinch would show us the treetops, where it loves to reside, and bids us seek an elevated perspective across the panorama of our lives. It urges us to listen in silence to the music of our soul, and tells us that we will reveal to ourselves the secret of our own soul music by noting those things that resonate with us – colours, the time of day, the phases of the Moon, the day of the week, the elements, sounds, flowers, cloud shapes, natural perfumes – all these things give intimations of the music of our individual soul, and by seeking them and appreciating them and actively using their potency, we will manifest our strength and creativity. The art of attaining broad perspective and the art of listening comprise the message of the hawfinch.

Lesser Redpoll: this little bird is associated with the feminine aspect of fire. We tend to think of fire as a purely masculine energy, and perhaps this imbalance is why the fiery principle within the human psyche is so often expressed in our world as a brutal, ruthless, conquering force, whether in business, politics, or international relations. Yet the truth about fire is that it is also a manifestation of the feminine principle. Brigid, once worshipped as the supreme goddess of the British Isles (erroneously thought to belong only to Ireland) is the guiding star of the wisdom of this little bird. As Divine Daughter, she bears the torch of the sacred and everlasting flame, and she wields it to enlighten our understanding. Her beautiful fire can be sensed most perfectly in the crimson of the dying day and the rose and golden flame of the rising Sun. The redpoll's message is: 'Burn brightly and gloriously in all your endeavours; but always remember the gentleness that is the strength in the heart of the flame, and that there is no need for your fires to wreak havoc and destruction at any level of life!'

Linnet (*see also individual entry*): the linnet bids us seek counsel from nature, to go out in it and observe it with our deeper selves. The linnet is a fairy bird, and the magic of nature and of the fairies is denoted by its presence. It bids us to reconnect with our child-self and to reignite our sense of wonder and play, especially in order to soothe destructive cravings and restlessness.

Scarlet Rosefinch: this singular little bird with its distinctive song bears the same message as the redpolls, only in the case of the rosefinch it aspects the feminine force, and advises us to work secretly, silently, unseen, from the fires of the heart and its intuition. The rosefinch, although a bird of spiritual fire, emphasizes water; and it is through the gentle, shielding medium of reflective water that the feminine principle pours its benediction of holy fire.

Scottish Crossbill: its augural meaning is the same as that of the crossbill, with the refinement that, in asserting ourselves positively in the outer world, we should seek to balance our actions by centring them in and calling them forth from meditative reflection and the calm contemplation of intuitive wisdom.

Serin: this tiny yellow finch comes to us when we are experiencing a battle, not between the heart and the head, but between the emotional, reactive, instinctive part of ourselves and the rule of the steadying mind. The serin advises that clear-headedness should be allowed to win the day. It also advises us to take charge of our thoughts, and to ensure that we keep them positive, kind and happy; if we take heed, the serin promises us a shower of little golden blessings.

Siskin: somewhat smaller than the greenfinch, the little siskin bears a similar message (*see* GREENFINCH *above*), but in this caser on a lighter, more playful note.

Twite: the twite's message is similar to that of the linnet (*see above*), with the specification that it comes to teach us to seek a balance between work and play, and to foster a feeling of playfulness and a tendency towards (kindly) laughter even in the midst of business and chores. It especially speaks to the overburdened and work-driven, and promises a calmer, healthier, more beautiful vitality in place of that generated by the old inner taskmaster for those who heed its bidding.

Firecrest

Hardly larger than the goldcrest, which is Britain and Ireland's smallest bird, the firecrest, together with the goldcrest, is associated with the magical story of the dart of Abaris. Abaris, the Scythian, was a devoted priest of Apollo. To reward him for his dedication, the Sun god gave him a golden arrow on which to ride through the heavens, so conveying on him the power of flight and mastery over the kingdoms of the air. This diminutive golden dart rendered him invisible; it was also endowed with the virtue of healing disease and illnesses of all kinds, and via its secret properties it enabled those into whose care it was given to utter oracles. Abaris entrusted this precious golden dart to Pythagorus before he died, and old texts proclaim that 'The dart of Abaris carried the philosopher wheresoever he desired it.' These little fiery-capped birds, the goldcrest and the firecrest, are associated with Abaris' golden dart and its magical properties.

If these delightful birds draw close to you, receive the golden dart that they signify into your heart, and be ready to receive thereby, perhaps from an unexpected source, an oracle, a healing benediction, and the opportunity to travel upon inner and outer spheres.

Flycatcher (Pied)

The pied flycatcher comes to you to indicate that the opportunity to make a choice is imminent. Its augural message further instructs that once you have made your decision, do not hesitate to implement it, and triumph will be yours. It is said that the sweet, somewhat plaintive song of this little bird can be interpreted as a mourning hymn to all lost causes and opportunities that might have been made good through decisive action, or as a poignant refrain of gladness that angel-proffered prospects have successfully been grasped, realized, and brought to fruition.

Flycatcher (Red-Breasted)

The augury of the red-breasted flycatcher is that an undeclared lover, or the opportunity to find a particular lover, is either present or about to enter your life, and that, if you wish to receive, return and consolidate this love, you are advised to seize the moment before it flies, never to return. The red-breasted flycatcher usually emphasizes an erotic involvement, but of course the love it predicts could apply to any arena.

Flycatcher (Spotted)

This little bird of woodland and mature gardens urges you to look closely into the events and situations of your life as its flow unfurls them in successive progression.

Is a pattern emerging, some mosaic or silhouette that is ready to fall into place in your perception? Some gift or trophy is ready to come to you as a benefit of recognizing this pattern. Read the encryption, and catch the revelation as it flies so that it will bring you reward and nourishment. The friendly little flycatcher will show you how if you allow your intuition to bring forth the answer to the puzzle that this little bird symbolizes. Its presence is a signature for hidden pictures and for assertive acceptance of the gift that their decipherment renders.

Fulmar

This seabird, smaller than the herring gull, foretells a meeting of old friends, or perhaps a bringing-together, from the far past, of devoted comrades or lovers who are ready to reunite in their present incarnation.

Its meaning is devotion, loyalty, and preservation of the flame of love amongst the endless tides of the vast and eternal ocean of time and being.

Gadwall (see DUCK)

Gannet

The gannet, larger and longer-necked than any member of the gull family, comes to deliver a message concerning the art of recharging. Its powerful wing beats, followed by effortless glides, show us how to express and conserve our energy. Until we learn this perfect balance, we will be subject to exhaustion, to being stopped in our tracks by the sudden descent of illness and mental and emotional burn-out, or by ineffectiveness and a general inability to cope.

The gannet has a hearty appetite, and it teaches us to feast well on what nourishes our lives. This nourishment incorporates what makes us feel good, what is personally important to us, what enables us to give, and, crucially, that method we prefer which enables us to withdraw from our outer lives into the life of the soul and the overlighting spirit, be it via meditation, gardening, walking in nature, or by availing ourselves of the masters of poetry, music or art. Common relaxation will not do. We have to go deeper, or, the gannet warns, we will find ourselves relying on mere mundane appetite to fill our needs, which leads to imbalances in our physical, mental and emotional lives.

The gannet cries, 'Feast well on every source that nourishes your life, drink deep of every pure well-spring, and you will free yourself from the tyranny of the forces of addiction and greed and all that demeans and disempowers the human spirit!'

Garganey

The garganey bears the same message as all members of the duck family (*see* DUCK), with the addition that it warns us that our emotions have either already backed up and spilled out into an area of our psyche that was not designed to bear the burden of them, or are in imminent danger of doing so. Just as rivers, seas, and still inland waters feed the surrounding land with their vapours and their mineral content and provide water for its occupants, but are not so helpful when they flood and drown the land, so it is with our own inner landscape. Sometimes, a seasonal flooding does provide nutrients for the land, and we may interpret this as an occasional emotional release, which is healthy and restorative. Continual flooding and standing water, however, bring impoverishment and malaise.

When the garganey comes to us (and there is a beautiful soothing music in the rhythm of its name), it urges us to find what will bring us calming, mastery and release of our critical emotional burden (perhaps a change of diet, a change of routine, more sleep, more fresh air, more silence, meditation, a handicraft, gentle exercise, a constructive, well-mediated confrontation, etc., etc.) and to thereby exchange the flood-warnings for an emotional containment that reflects the waters of peace and well-being deep within the soul.

Godwit (Bar-Tailed)

The bar-tailed godwit bears the same augury as the black-tailed godwit, except that in this case it prophesies that the spiritual feminine principle, the Great Mother-God who is all and contains all, will open the eyes of your soul to her magical presence. Prepare to receive the Paraclete, the breath of the Holy Spirit, indescribably sweet.

Godwit (Black-Tailed)

The clue to the godwit's augury is in its name, for despite the vagaries behind the bestowment of it, this elegant, long-beaked wader bids us seek knowledge and witness of God, of the spirit, of our deeper selves. We need not put a name to the unnamable, or a gender, or any human construction at all if we are not at ease with such concepts; yet those who seriously consult an oracle are likely to agree that there is a presence beyond the outer world that we experience materially with our five senses. Nevertheless, the aspect of God which will be revealed to you will tend to elucidate the spiritual masculine principle, the all-loving Father.

When the godwit steps daintily into your life, its arrival foretells that a veil is to be lifted from your vision so that you can draw closer to spirit, to God. This is a beautiful augury, and will surely bring joy to anyone who receives it.

Goldcrest (see also FIRECREST)

When this little wonder-bird takes flight into your life, you are invited to make a wish. The remainder of its augury is the same as for its cousin, the firecrest.

Goldeneye (see also DUCK)

The goldeneye's message is similar to that given by the duck, although it confirms that you have indeed 'hit the mark' in achieving a harmonious and creative inflow and outflow of balanced emotion, and that you will reap the golden bounty belonging to the attainment of such a state.

Golden Plover

There is a strange Icelandic legend which says that as boys, Christ and his playmates amused themselves by fashioning bird shapes out of clay. A Sadducee passed by, and, outraged because it was the Sabbath, broke the diminutive clay models. Christ at once blessed the little broken birds, and they were changed into golden plovers which took to the wing, crying 'Glory! Glory!' as they flew. Since then, says the folktale, they have given voice to the same cry, and will do so until the world ends.

The sweet, unearthly whistling of the golden plover reminds us of the blessing which is brought forth by sorrow. If the innocent handiwork of the children had not been broken, it would never have received its blessing and would have remained lifeless clay.

The golden plover's cry says to us: 'Whatever becomes crystallized must be broken to release the splendour of the imprisoned life within!'

Goldfinch (see FINCH)

Goosander (see also DUCK)

The goosander brings an augury which is the same as that of the duck, with the addition that it foretells the coming of a sweet, poignant, nostalgic tide into your emotional life, which will awaken magical memories of childhood and perhaps even evocative moments from past lives. These recollections come to balance, harmonize and reintegrate the different facets of your life, and to set free the well-springs in your soul.

Goose

Falsely held up as a symbol of foolishness, the wise and shrewd goose is a bird of the Goddess, fiercely maternal and protective in its habits.

This knowing bird has been blessed with an abundance of years, attaining the age of thirty when allowed to do so. It is also a symbol of productivity and fertility and is fabled to lay the golden egg. This indicates that it is a solar bird, because the feast of the winter solstice, the return of the Sun, was traditionally the goose-feast, both before and after it became Christianized.

The greylag goose mates for life, and so the goose signifies fidelity. Its maternal aggressiveness made it an emblem of battle in the ancient past. Iron-age warriors were often buried with geese, and in Brittany a bronze figurine of a Celtic war-goddess has been discovered, bearing a helmet surmounted by a goose in combative posture.

The vigilant goose often makes itself noticed as an angelic messenger when we need a vote of confidence to be spurred on to initiate something – a marriage or committed relationship, a family, a business, a business amalgamation, a spiritual group, an artistic or creative project, the birth of a new friendship, the establishment of a home.

It was the egg of a goose which Mary Magdalene brought to the Roman emperor Tiberius a year after the Crucifixion in order to bring him tidings of the message of the Christ. Tiberius listened to her words with respect, but remarked that he could no more believe in the Resurrection than he could be expected to believe that the goose egg she held could suddenly turn red, upon which the egg turned bright crimson. This miracle of the goose egg initiated Mary's great teaching mission, recorded in contemporaneous documents which state that hundreds of thousands flocked to her visionary, beautifully-spoken, kindly sermons and were baptized by her in the waters of Glastonbury, formerly known as Avalon.

The goose says: 'Initiate, consolidate, move forward! It is time to establish, and to serve and nourish what you establish! The powers of heaven are with you, to fill your vessel and to guard it!'

Goose (Barnacle) *(see individual entry and also* GOOSE*)*

Goose (Bean) *(see also* GOOSE*)*

This is a goose of the Otherworld, denoting magic, enchantment, women's mysteries and the luck of the fairies. When you are brought into the presence of the bean goose, you may be due to receive a message from the spirit worlds, to be given a revelation concerning nature's magical inner sanctum, or to receive an initiation from the fairies.

The message of the bean goose is: 'Ask, and you shall receive!' However, it is important to understand that this exhortation relates to spiritual and psychic gifts and concerns, and does not involve materialism.

Goose (Brent) *(see also* GOOSE*)*

The brent goose encourages us to move forward in lofty and arduous enterprises which are motivated by high aspiration. It cries: 'Press on, press on! The gods, the angels, and Divine Spirit are with you!'

Goose (Canada) *(see also* GOOSE*)*

The Canada goose brings us some form of medicine from the Otherworld. In the shamanic sense, its good medicine comes to heal and transform the 'bad medicine' in a life. What is the 'bad medicine'? The Canada goose will help us to identify both the bad medicine and its antedote. Sometimes, there is no specific 'bad' medicine, and its gift is simply one of transfigurative blessing.

The Canada goose alerts us to these truths and, if we allow ourselves to take flight with it and to be borne forward on its soul currents (which means allowing ourselves to respond intuitively to its assistance via our imagination), it will guide us to the good medicine waiting to enlighten us.

Goose (Egyptian) *(see also* GOOSE*)*

The Egyptian goose tells us to follow the Sun, not in a recreational sense, but as the star by which to steer our course. When we follow the Sun, we live by our highest aspirations and our most far-sighted principles, and walk always towards the light.

The Egyptian goose signifies that we have arrived at the point where no other path through life will satisfy us. The grand and glorious call to follow the Sun can be applied to little events and humble situations as well as to the sweeping panorama of the royal highway of our life. In reminding us of this, the Egyptian goose also sounds a warning. In taking up the challenge to follow the Sun, arrogance may waylay us, tempting us to think that our personal interpretation of what is right and good is the only one, and that the glory we perceive and strive after is actually emanating from us as a personal attribute!

The Egyptian goose calls: 'Follow the Sun, let your light shine, but root yourself in humility!'

Goose (Greylag) *(see also* GOOSE*)*

This is often the goose that appears in fairytales, which always have profound lessons to impart. If we think of the story of the goose girl, we note that she was nobly born but banished by evil forces from her true home, and set to mind the geese. What have we within ourselves that was given to us to set to a noble purpose, and yet we allow circumstances to lock us into a position where we use it only for menial and uninspired purposes?

The cry of the wild greylag goose calls to that divine wildness within us which throws off convention and the shackles of commonplace, stultified vision. It urges us to refuse to be a common denominator, and to make the great escape to a nobler destiny!

Goose (Pink-Footed) *(see also* GOOSE*)*

This pink-footed member of the clan bears the same general message as the goose, but through the roseate tinge of romance. When this goose declares its presence, a romantic involvement or an emotionally regenerating friendship is likely to be on the horizon. It advises you not so much to look at life through a rose-tinted lens, but rather to root and ground yourself in the beautiful promise of the rose, symbol of the loving heart, which will open your heart and allow you to give and receive the blessing of love.

Goose (Snow) (see also GOOSE)

This beautiful bird with its evocative cry and its polar whiteness of the wild north is a symbol of purity, of the sublime. It signifies what we truly are when our soul flies free and we have released ourselves from the stains and petty mundane claims of the burdening Earth. We are emanations from a vast, wild and pure heart, eternally beating in unbroken rhythm.

When the snow goose draws near to you, it comes to remind you that you have forgotten who you truly are, and to reawaken that sleeping remembrance so that you might be empowered and filled with the supreme conviction that the heights, the glories, the peaks of attainment belong to you, and that you are an intrepid voyager of the stars.

Goose (White Domestic) (see also GOOSE)

The message of the white domestic fowl is the same as the goose augury, except that it also emphasizes the need for protection. It tells you that you are indeed protected by angels, by the light of the Divine, and by your own light, which partakes of the nature of the latter.

The spirit goose itself protects you. But you may additionally need more mundane protection at this time – perhaps psychic protection, which you will receive from visualizing yourself in the centre of a circle of glorious light, or the protection of numbers so that you are not alone, or the protection of caution, where you are careful not to put yourself in danger. Medical protection and precaution may be necessary, the protection of locks and bolts, legal protection, or the protection of your own vulnerability, either psychological or physical.

Remember, though, that the white goose's message is *protection* rather than danger. Respond to its warning, and all will be well. Its message may concern the need for you to offer protection to someone else, or to be aware that someone in your care may require it. If you are confused about the nature of the protection you need to put in place, you may like to use further augury and your own inner listening to divine it.

Goose (White-Fronted) *(see also* GOOSE)

This goose speaks to us of the Abode of Joy, which is the third eye or brow chakra. It encourages us to seek laughter and to express laughter in our lives, to feel the real surge of joyful, effervescent energy that rises in us like a fountain when we truly see the funny side of events. This bird is the bird of heart-sourced mirth.

Goshawk *(see also* HAWK)

The majestic goshawk bears, with the general augury of the hawk, the message that a quest, a challenge, an adventure is about to come into your life, and that you will need to use all of your inner resources to hunt down your quarry and make it your own.

If a man is visited by the goshawk, it urges him to look to his knightly qualities or to his higher nature, and that he will need the help of a woman to fulfill his quest.

When the goshawk draws close to a woman, it indicates, in addition to the augury cited above, that a man of knightly virtues will be available to help her triumph in her quest.

Great Tit *(see* BLUE TIT)

Grebe

The grebe emphasizes the dynamic within relationships.

Black-necked Grebe: this pretty little waterfowl tells of the need for a 'heart-to-heart' between lovers or friends, so that the voyage of your friendship or love affair might not be hindered, suffer mutiny, or turned off course. Its lonely call among the rushes sings of the need for times of solitude and personal space within relationships, but its plaintive poignancy also warns against retreating from the intimacy enshrined within them, and withdrawing from the magnetism that first drew you together. The voice within the reeds is the voice that tells secrets; the black-necked grebe comes to us to urge us to continue sharing them with those we love.

Great Crested Grebe: this largest of the grebes, with its prominent crest, speaks to us of the need for the demonstration and verbalization of affection and appreciation within our relationships, administered with royal grace.

Little Grebe: smallest of the grebes, this little water bird conveys the wisdom of protecting our relationships. Many fine strands are woven into creating them; subtle and delicate, they can become tangled and even broken if we allow the inundation of the coarser emotions to take over in our interaction. Irritation, intolerance, allowing resentments to fester, the temptation to brush aside or dismiss one another's views and contributions, the need to psychologically score over the other person, all of these everyday and apparently trivial insensitivities can slowly starve and disenchant a relationship. The little grebe bids us strenuously defend our relationships from the predators within us.

Red-necked Grebe: the augury of this larger grebe is to use passion wisely within our relationships. The nature of passion is movement and rest; if we understand this rhythm, we can ride its tides with mastery and release.

Slavonian Grebe: The striking Slavonian grebe bears an augury concerning gifts and ceremony in friendships and love relationships. To create a feeling of occasion, to honour a loved one, is an important part of the unspoken dialogue between partners and friends. Dedication of time and exclusive focus are a form of gift-giving and ceremony.

Greenfinch (see FINCH)

Greenshank

The greenshank speaks of heart-motivated penetration of the sublime spheres so that gifts of the spirit might be brought back to Earth and given freely to those inhabiting the mundane planes of consciousness. Whether these perpendicular flights are taken via art or insight, they are always visionary, and are sometimes ecstatic. However blithe their ascent may be, there is always some danger in their dramatic descent. If you are among these chosen ones, these Promethean-like souls who rise to great heights to secrete the miracle of the fire of the gods in your consciousness so that you may bring it back to Earth to enlighten, inspire and scintillate those around you, you may sometimes suffer from depression, exhaustion and hopelessness simply because of the pressure of your spiritual missions.

The greenshank reminds us of the greatest manifestation of greenery in fairytale and myth – that of the beanstalk! We remember how Jack (a generic name for 'Everysoul' who has awakened to their spiritual gifts and their true mission in life) advanced straight upwards into the heaven worlds, and through his bravery and spiritual aptitude descended just as steeply with the giant's treasure. The giant (the gods) pursued Jack hotly, wanting the price of death and engorgement as his due for what Jack had claimed from the heavens. Jack saved himself with one simple act – he cut down the beanstalk!

The greenshank, who carries the mark of the arrowhead and is associated with the Sagittarian gods of learning and the fiery arrow of exalted consciousness, aimed straight at the mark of highest heaven, bids us follow Jack's example. Once we have brought back the treasure from on high, we should seal off our means of access, in case entities hostile to our questing adventures pursue us. This means simply closing down; after meditation, after spiritual flight or progress 'up the beanstalk' via deep communion with our higher selves through any means of exertion, we need to ground ourselves by taking a moment to imagine great roots growing in strength from our feet and anchoring us firmly and safely into the Earth. We need to place the mental image of a circle of light containing a cross of light over our crown centre (the top of the head), our brow centre (on the brow ridge between the eyes) the throat centre (in the hollow of the throat), the heart centre (in the middle of the chest) and the solar plexus centre. In this way, we cut down our beanstalk until such time as we decide to cast our magic beans once more to the winds of the spirit and allow it to grow again. Thereby we can assure that the angry giant has no access to ourselves or our world, and cannot make us suffer for our heroic retrievals!

Grouse (Black) (see also CAPERCAILLIE)

The message of the black grouse is similar to that of the capercaillie, except that it emphasizes the hidden song of the wild. Strange sights, strange fairy music, have been heard and seen on lonely moors. The black grouse bids us open our soul to hidden beauties, secret mysteries. It also bids us beware of the Fairy Terror. If, when we are near fairy haunts, we fail to express the required soul sensitivities to mysterious presences, the Terror can fall on us. This often-reported phenomenon is characterized by an entirely causeless horror that takes imperative and irresistible hold. The victim, however rational or fearless an individual, can only flee in dread, running for never-before-achieved distances before the overriding panic subsides!

If we are experiencing fear and panic in our lives and the black grouse makes itself known to us, we are drawing near to some secret cavern within which, if its treasure is won, will unfold a great beauty, a mysterious jewel of the soul. Our fear lets us know that we are approaching the shrine of this great gift in the wrong way, without calling on the soul wisdom and range of sensitivities within us which will enable us to victoriously receive this jewel.

The black grouse can bring an otherworldly music to our inner ear which will help us to overcome our limitations. Sit in meditation and let the spirit presence of this bird guide you.

Grouse (Red)
(see also CAPERCAILLIE and GROUSE (BLACK))

The red grouse bears a like augury to that of the capercaillie and the black grouse, but, in the case of this bird, it sounds an alert to retrace our steps because we have missed something. This missed treasure will be of a kind with the secret, inner wealth which its two grouse cousins emphasize. When the red grouse makes its presence known to us, we have been blind and deaf to a precious gift which called to us without avail as we passed its way. The red grouse's call is literally: 'Go-back, back, back, go-back!'

Guillemot
(N. America: Common Murre)

This seabird speaks to us of the rock-like qualities of life. It reassures us that we can stand straight, firm, and steadfast against life's storms and temptations. Long-lived and wise, the guillemot reminds us that the wonders of the cosmos include the mineral people, the fairy and spirit intelligences within stone, who are individuals just as we are, and experience their world as airy and spacious, as we experience ours.

The sagacious guillemot, which stands tall and upright in its rocky home and which was reared as a chick directly on the rock-face, with no nest separating it from its mineral guardian, bids us reach out in spirit to these intelligences. We have much to learn from them, and their calm immovability can be our own, vouchsafed as their blessing, in times of crisis and pressure.

Guillemot (Black)

The black guillemot speaks to us of our roots, our origins. This cousin of the true guillemot, nests in caves, sometimes drawing close to human communities and building its nest in harbour walls and other man-made constructions. It tells us that our ancestors have some meaningful message to impart.

If the black guillemot makes itself known to you, look to your place of birth and the history of your bloodline. Look deep into yourself as a continuity of it. What ancestral spirits walk with you today?

The black guillemot's keening whistle declares: 'What is in your roots has a gift to give to your conscious awareness!'

Gull (see SEAGULL)

Harrier (Hen) (see also HAWK)

The hen harrier comes to us to lift us out of the limitations of petty and domestic concerns. It cries: 'You hold the gifts of higher vision and broader horizons in your own hands!'

Harrier (Marsh) (see also HAWK)

This bird of prey urges us to rise above an emotional inscape which is sucking under our vital attributes and sundering us from our flow of opportunities and the potential within us that seizing them would unlock. It may be grief, heartbreak, sorrow concerning the past, remorse, disappointment, abandonment, attachment to something lost, disenchantment, the pain of denial, shame, resentment, fear and self-doubt, or even self-pity. Whatever it is, the marsh harrier has appeared in your life to be kindly but drastic!

Its wailing cry affirms: 'It is not the end of the story! Write the next chapter with renewed verve and vigour and you will change the past through your new perspective!'

Harrier (Montagu's) (*see also* HAWK)

Montagu's harrier indicates that, if we carefully nourish the foundation of our projects, relationships, or whatever it is we are concerned with when it makes itself known to us, we will attain the highest peaks of success or experience.

Hawfinch (*see* FINCH)

Hawk

This dignified bird teaches us of spiritual quest, true pride, nobility and stature. It is also associated with recollection, cleansing, and the granting, or urging, of a detailed, aerial hawk's-eye view of our lives, and the stitches of that tapestry which comprise our current situation. The hawk connects us with our roots, for there is in this bird the spirit of ancestry.

The ancient druidical bards were known to cherish 'bird's knowledge' within their tradition. Their priests donned mantles of feathers for the performance of special rites, and auguries were read by observing the flight and habits of birds. The Druid entered the worlds within, and there called to him his totem bird to lead him safely deep into the spirit realms.

From earliest times, preceding and including the first Egyptians, the nobility or chieftains of ancient tribes hunted with hawks. In the chivalric age of medieval Europe, kings, princes, dukes, earls, counts and barons used falcons, whilst yeomen used goshawks ('A kestrel for a knave' is the final line of a traditional rhyme). Ladies hunted with the smallest of the hawk family, the enigmatic little merlin. For priests and all men of the cloth, the sparrowhawk was the specified bird that accompanied them on the hunt.

When the hawk appears to you, or hovers above you in the air, bathe the eyes of your inner vision in its pristine energies of the upper air, look out upon the grand design of your life, and know that you are rooted in your ancestral soul in all its greatness and spiritual munificence.

Hear the hawk say: 'My scream is the trumpet of the herald! Be alert! You are about to receive heaven's grace in shadow or shine, and the tide of spirit-messages to help you unlock your gift is already thundering on your shores!'

Heron (Grey) (also CRANE)

The heron signifies time, longevity, focused patience, untiring concentration and secret knowledge. It also symbolizes fertility, therapeutic forgetting, children and regeneration. Heron plumes are a symbol of silence. It is a bird sacred to morning because, standing in the water or the shallows of the sea, it is the first to greet the dawn.

Legend tells of a lonely heron dwelling on an isle off the coast of County Mayo in Ireland, who has lived there since the beginning of the world, and who will remain until the end of time.

In ancient Egypt it was the bird of writing and writers, and in the druidic tradition, as keeper of secret knowledge it was associated with the Ogham script, a language of runes founded on a tree-alphabet. It is noteworthy that in our culture, the tree (paper) has provided us with our written and printed knowledge through books. The pages of a book are still called its 'leaves', and the tree is, of course, the home and procreative shelter of birds; the bird is almost the tree's singing, darting spirit, its aerial daemon, as trees are said to have also their own hidden spirit which are creatures of the ether, yet bound to their roots.

As birds of the water, the heron is a bird of the subconscious, of concealed depths, and so it reveals itself as a bird of the Moon, said to wax and wane with the lunar light. It shares the darkness of Saturn, that wise old god of time who knows how to restrain and imprison until the time is right to grant release. The baby, confined in the darkness of the waters of the womb until it is ready to be born, is a perfect symbol of the wisdom of Saturn, and of the patience of the heron as it stands motionless in the water for hours on end, not absent or dreaming or lethargic, but focused, actively concentrating. When it spies the shadow of a swift-moving fin, it darts with the speed of an arrow at its prey, and emerges triumphant.

When the heron comes to you, think of these things. Do you need patience to bring a scheme to fruition? Perhaps your life seems flat and constricted, and the heron is bringing you a message to say that the fish will soon appear, or the child of your perseverance and sacrifice will soon make itself known to you. The heron brings many messages, and for writers or those who work with language, it comes as an ally, ever inspiring us to bring forth deeper language-magic from the fathomless, dark pool of the creative subconscious.

Its rasping cry brings us the message: 'There is a time for all things, and a season for every purpose under the Sun.'

Heron (Night) *(see also* HERON (GREY))

The night heron, active at dawn and dusk and throughout the watches of the night, brings us wise dreams. Its crouching posture, when roosting, merges its head into its body, showing us that, like the sacred disembodied heads that the Druids revered, it symbolizes elevated consciousness. The ancient idea of baptism stems in part from the concept that the head must go under and rise again, because all entities, whatever their element, draw the fluidity of perception and vision, which we call consciousness, from the mysterious depths of the water.

The forces of chaos are said to dwell in deep water, and from this rich life-stream, esotericists say, we draw to us those components we need to build our own inner cosmos, absorbing them into ourselves, through our own soul-attunement and differentiation, so that they transform into beautiful ordered symphonies of inspired design. Thus is the cosmos (meaning 'beautiful order') of consciousness and of the outer worlds ever formed and forged anew, self-created by God and by God's creature, the human being.

Dreaming is an important aspect of this method of selection and self-creation, and so we take care to listen to the dreams to which the night heron draws our attention. They are vital in our great task of self-creation. This ancient, dreaming bird that signifies the sage will help us to decipher their portents, revelations, emphases and deeper meaning.

Heron (Purple) *(see also* HERON (GREY))

Although it is smaller than the grey heron, the purple heron is recognized in folklore as the royal heron. Its snake-like neck links it with the feathered serpent, the sign of esoteric knowledge and revelation. It comes as a portent of healing, and will guide us to a path leading to a renewal of health and wholeness.

Heron (White) *(see* EGRET (LITTLE) and also HERON (GREY))

Hobby *(see also* HAWK)

Sometimes called the robber hawk because it snatches seized prey from the clutch of others of its species, the hobby is fast and powerful in flight. It is possible that the 'dapple-dawn-drawn Falcon' which inspired Gerard Manley Hopkins to immortalize it in 'The Windhover' was a hobby rather than a kestrel because of the hobby's impressive 'stationary' flight and its breathtaking aerial turns. It is interesting to consider in relation to Hopkins' deep spiritual insight into the falcon or hawk – identifying it with Christ – that the ancient Egyptians believed that the skies were a vast falcon in flight, with the Sun and the Moon as its right and left eye.

The hobby, in conjunction with the general augury of the hawk, tells us that there is some spiritual trophy, some soul-realization or culmination that we must seize. An opportunity must not be lost, but must be translated into tangible currency that will enrich and ennoble your life. The hobby does not, of course, counsel us to rob! Yet if a special opportunity arises and you can dare to be the first to seize it, then you will have won the day, and the fates – including the spirit of the hobby – will smile on you.

The hobby's motto is, without too narrow an interpretation: 'Faint heart never won fair maiden!'

Hoopoe

This striking, exotic bird was revered as sacred by all the ancient Egyptians. It was placed on the sceptre of Horus, the falcon god who represented exalted consciousness or the divine single eye of God. The hoopoe symbolized joy and filial affection; in the wider sense, the love of the supreme God for all the human family as well as the entire family of creation, and the deity's delight in it. The hoopoe was especially venerated by the Egyptians because of its impressive 'sun-crest' which it raises when alert; its upper markings which when in flight are strangely reminiscent of Egyptian art; and the 'winged ayin' or sacred eye, like one 'V' on top of another, which can be seen clearly delineated in buff-gold on its folded wings. Its soft, low, musical call of 'hoop-hoop' resonates over wide distances, and is said to sound the sacred word or name of a deity.

In Greek legend, the hoopoe is given a sorrowfully poignant designation as the bird which had once lived on Earth as a Thracian king, Tereus, who had sought to murder two sisters, Philomela and Procne. He had married Procne and ravished Philomela, cutting out her tongue so that she could not speak of his terrible deed. Philomela nevertheless managed to communicate his crime to Procne by weaving a tapestry of her tragic story for her sister, and so the king decided to silence them both forever. Before he could perpetrate the double murder, his wife Procne, driven to an act of insanity by her husband's abuses, put to death her own son and served him as a dish for Tereus, unwittingly, to eat. The gods, to put an end to the grim drama, transformed Philomela into a nightingale, Procne into a swallow, and the Thracian king into a hoopoe, that the continual utterance of the sacred word sounded by this royal, crested bird would cleanse his soul of its degradation and restore to him a sense of the sacredness of the family circle, so utterly abominated by his deeds and their dire influence.

The augural meaning of the hoopoe combines its divine auspice, given above, with the message that your prayers will be answered, and that you will be led into the healing sanctuary of your own family, whether this family consists of conventional blood-ties or exclusively of subtle soul-links.

Ibis or Nile-Bird

The ancient Egyptians' title of reverence for the sacred ibis was Father John. It was the avatar of the god Thoth, known later as Hermes in Greece, which was the Egyptian name for Enki or Oannes (*see entry under* LAPWING), he who gave the divine Hermetic or Zoroastrian wisdom-teachings to humankind. Enki, the John-man (called by future generations 'the Wise Knight' or the first 'Gentle Man'), was still fighting the good fight in Egypt on behalf of humanity against his evil-intentioned brother Enlil, known to the Egyptians as Seth or Typhon. In the guise of an ibis, Enki or Thoth escaped the murderous pursuit of Enlil or Typhon.

The ibis, avatar of Enki or Thoth, represents the initial letter of the Egyptian alphabet, and is a sigil of the origin of language and all that civilizes humankind. The Egyptians maintained that the white plumage of the ibis symbolizes the light of the Sun, its black neck the shadow of the Moon or the sacred darkness, its body a heart, and its legs a triangle. It was said to drink only the purest of water, and that its feathers would scare or even kill the mighty crocodile, which is an emblem of Enlil in the full power and wrath of his lower saurian mentality or what is known esoterically as the Dragon of Earth, which corresponds to the baser self, the 'Mr Hyde' within human consciousness. (Both Enlil and Enki, even though they were human beings who lived on Earth, albeit superhumans dwelling in a higher dimension of our planet than the dimension of its physical atoms, were of a race known as the Serpent People.)

It is further said of the ibis that its essence is so woven into the fabric of the soul of Egypt that it would pine to death if transported elsewhere – a poetical rather than a literal truth underlining Enki's devotion to the principles of human civilization and spiritual progress (Enlil, in contradistinction, wished to see humanity degenerate into brutishness and destroy itself.) The ibis, truly a manifestation of the magical soul of ancient Egypt, appears at the rise of the Nile, but disappears at its inundation, as though this abundant overflow of enriching waters was its gift and its new form. It was in ancient times a crime to kill or injure the sacred bird, which was believed to feed on serpents' eggs, symbols of divine wisdom.

If the ibis draws close to you, a spiritual call is sounding your name. You have been chosen to enter into a new and elevated spiritual understanding. The lonely cry of the Bird of Thoth is a call to your heart: 'I offer Enlightenment.'

Jackdaw

The divine fool comes to us through the jackdaw. It can bring a blessing of prosperity and happiness, or it can signify what is imitative and lacking in substance and sincerity. If the jackdaw makes its presence known to you, check your connection with your heart-consciousness. If it is flowing peacefully and unimpeded, the jackdaw bestows a light-hearted benediction. If not, it sounds an alarm-call. This auspice suggests overall the inner reflection and discernment pertaining to the dynamic of wisdom, and wisdom is the theme of the black bird, whether of carrion or otherwise.

They are universally associated with the sacred feminine and with Goddess, and linked with death and decay, not because of anything inherent in their spiritual reality, but because of the death and decay attending the planetary cultural, social, psychological and psychic understanding of, and resultant attitudes towards, the divine feminine principle.

The jackdaw promises felicity and prosperity in marriage if a bride-to-be meets it on her wedding morning. The touch of grey about the jackdaw's head associates it further with wisdom and the knowledge of ancient secrets and lost knowledge. Women, especially old wives and wise women, were once thought to understand the jackdaw's speech. A reference in William of Malmesbury's *Kings of England* (1042) tells of a woman who, on hearing a jackdaw chattering and scolding volubly, turned pale and declared that some terrible calamity lay in wait for her.

A solitary jackdaw that keeps returning in spite of attempts to scare it away is a sign that the bird is sounding a solemn warning. A report in a Gloucestershire newspaper of 1873 relates an incident involving a jackdaw at the time of a fatal misadventure on the site of a suspension bridge over the Avon. At the point during the construction when the river was spanned simply by a single chain, many of the workmen had commented upon the fact that a solitary jackdaw sat immovably at its centre. The phenomenon had been widely regarded as a precursor of ill luck, but unfortunately the construction team took no action regarding the omen, and, sure enough, it was followed by the death of one of their number shortly afterwards.

There are many such stories and reports, and it is difficult to determine why the jackdaw (along with other black birds) is considered an 'evil' bird when it offers such thoughtfully-staged warnings, within a time span that easily enables its recipients to act on the given omens and so avert the prophesied disaster. It is surely quite the opposite; and its status as fosterer of Goddess wisdom was celebrated in many districts by men who were careful to salute the jackdaw by removing their hats in respectful salute.

. If, in coming to you, this bird seems to sound a warning, never take it in the spirit of doleful, gloomy inevitability. The jackdaw wishes you to beware, and to transform the outcome it prophesies into a happier one. However, its message is far more likely to be one of discernment, as outlined above.

Jay

The jay's poor reputation in relatively recent folklore results from a blunder in comprehension. The bird was said to represent a wanton, a simpleton, a fool who spends his money recklessly. In fact the appellation springs merely from the letter 'J', the initial letter of an unfortunate by the name of Juggins who in 1887 became famous for making a fool of himself due to his highly frequent and drastic losses on the turf!

It has nothing to do with this brightly-coloured bird of the woodlands which adroitly and beautifully serves Mother Earth by planting oak forests. It does so by making underground stores of acorns, which it loves to eat. Nevertheless, the acorns are planted at intervals which, mysteriously, perfectly minister to the requirements of the young saplings.

It is a bird of regeneration, associated with the oak and the priest of the oak, the Druid. To carry jay's feathers in your pocket is said to bring good luck, prosperity and long life. It is a bird of Jupiter, the Lord of Form. It comes to you when you need to manifest something in your life, or perhaps when what is manifest needs to be restructured or even deconstructed. Its message may be simply that you need more structure to your life, your time, your project, your relationship.

Its harsh scream commands: 'Build your dream! Embody your ideal! Anchor your vision!'

Kestrel (*see also* HAWK)

The kestrel denotes humility in pride. It comes to remind us of this necessary soul-stance whenever we find ourselves in a position of authority, or achieve notable success, or are given the gift of good luck, as in winning a big sum of money.

The kestrel teaches that true humility will safeguard us as we take joy in gliding and soaring like the majestic hawk which ecstatically treads the upper air. Its laughing call ('kee-kee-kee') bids us laugh at ourselves and our conceits.

Kingfisher

The lovely Greek legend of the kingfisher tells of Queen Halcyone, who awaited the return of her king, Ceyx of Trachis, with untiring faith and patience. One night, his death at sea by drowning was revealed to her in a dream. In an agony of grief, she rushed down to the seashore and flung herself into the waves where his drowned body was floating. The gods, looking on from Olympus, took pity on her, and, as a reward for her fidelity, transformed the king and queen into a pair of kingfishers, whose souls were bound to the waters and who would always be faithful to one mate.

This fidelity and devotion and its association with water also suggests the Arthurian Fisher King who, according to esoteric interpretation, lies wounded and grieving because his beloved has been brutally torn away from him and ejected into banishment and impenetrable shadow. Because the Fisher King is a symbol of humanity and humanity's source, the kingfisher myth suggests what will happen on a worldwide scale when the Fisher King and his bride are at last reunited.

The gods further decreed that those days upon which the kingfishers sat on their eggs and raised their young would be calm, fair-weather days when there would be no storms at sea. This gave rise to the tradition of the 'halcyon days', days of tranquil and beautiful weather.

That the kingfisher is a bird denoting the spiritual significance of bright blue skies and golden sunshine is further confirmed in another myth, which says that during the Flood, Noah let it out of the Ark, whereupon it flew so high that its formerly grey plumage took on the cerulean blue of the sky, and its nearness to the Sun gave it its red breast and rear feathers. These feathers, if carried or worn, were believed to impart the blessings of averting thunder and lightning-strike, revealing hidden treasure, and bestowing grace and beauty on the wearer.

These virtues are woven into its wider augury, so that those who receive it are destined to be peace-makers, to bring forth the best in people and situations, and to walk in a golden aura which will augment their inner and outer loveliness. It is indeed a bird of happy omen, favoured by the gods, and brings affirmation of a sunny, serene period coming into a life, within which it would be well to originate any project, undertaking or soul-change in need of protection and nurturing in its early stages.

The kingfisher is also associated with showing which way the wind is blowing, which further marks its appearance as a sign that an opportunity worth grasping will soon appear. It is also a bird of purity and incorruptibility, and its appearance either confirms purity of motive, or questions it as a warning.

Kite (Red) (see also HAWK)

The kite, seen sailing high in the air, foretells long, hot, tranquil summer days. This weather prophecy extends to its general augury. It also urges us to let go of what might be too tight a grip on material and mundane concerns, and to allow ourselves to float nearer to heaven. As in the concept of the sacred and ceremonial Chinese kite, we are reminded that as we walk our daily path through life, we should hold firmly to the kite-string which connects our soul to heaven.

Kittiwake (*see also* SEAGULL)

The kittiwake bears the same augury as other seagulls, except that its message prophesies the advent of an adventure of the heart. There is a wild, even ferocious quality to the seagull which is gentler and more romantic in the case of the kittiwake. It is the 'dove' of the seagull race.

Knot

This seabird, which changes its plumage from a speckled soft mist-grey to a glowing terracotta during the summer, is distinguished by the balletic aerial displays of its flocks. It calls to you that something veiled within your psyche, something unseen and perhaps even unwittingly ignored by you, is urgently seeking expression; some quality of mind or soul needs an outlet. If you have been feeling off-colour at any level recently, this underlying need for something within you to manifest itself may be the cause. Your own wisdom will delineate it for you, of course; but it is likely to be some beautiful gift of creativity that you never suspected was a part of you. It may be something simple, such as the ability to bake cakes that delight people, or to create a sanctuary within the garden or the home – or it may be something more dramatically life-changing. It is also likely to be associated with the sacred feminine, with creative, birthing forces operating on many levels.

The message of this bird also counsels you to undertake the development of your stirring gift within the company of like-minded others so that you can benefit from a support network. It is worth remembering that the Celtic knot is a beautiful symbol of love expressing itself throughout eternity within the configurations of the human brain, human consciousness.

The knot is therefore an ancient symbol of the sacred feminine, or love-wisdom – the mounting light that embraces in spirals – manifesting in all aspects of life. It is especially an esoteric symbol of Mary

Magdalene. Perhaps this casts light on the negative expression of the knot, such as is experienced through a 'knotty' problem or a choking of the life-forces in some way. When this happens, the divine love-wisdom within us is somehow not being allowed to mount its heavenly stairway and so circulate the spiritual light throughout the configurations of our being as it should. The idea of the knot in wrong manifestation, not operating in accordance with its sacred design and so creating a point of stress rather than radiance, is incorporated in a parable from ancient Persia:

> Once upon a time the fishes of a certain river took counsel together and said: 'They tell us that our life and being is from the water, but we have never seen water, and know not what it is.'
>
> Then some among them wiser than the rest said: 'We have heard that there dwelleth in the sea a very learned fish that knoweth all things; let us ask him to explain to us what is water.'
>
> So several of their number set out, and came to where this sage fish resided. On hearing their request he answered them thus:
>
>> O ye who seek to solve the knot!
>> Ye live in God, yet know him not!
>> Ye sit upon the river's brink,
>> Yet crave in vain a drop to drink.
>> Ye dwell beside a countless store,
>> Yet perish hungry at the door.

This, without the slightly ranting note, is what the knot seeks to convey! You are sourced in your own riches, yet you cannot release their abundance. Trust in a higher guidance to show you the way forward, and consult with the knot, for this wise bird of the sea will bear light to your soul. The knot's cry is a high-pitched 'quick-ick' as it takes flight, for it is calling with its spirit-influences to quicken something deep within you into manifest life.

Lapwing

In Celtic lore the lapwing is associated with Bran, god of the underworld and keeper of secrets. The lapwing's sacred task was to disguise the secret, in company with the hound, whose task was to guard it, and the roebuck, whose duty was to hide it in his thicket; thus the 'enemy' – the ignorant or ill-willed – could not maraud and violate this precious secret knowledge. So it is that the lapwing is said to cry 'Bewitched! Bewitched!' for her esoteric mission is to bewitch, to disguise, to confuse. She bears the key to the portals of revelation but only if you can first answer her wisdom-testing riddles.

To the Druids she was the bird of magic and poetry.

The mystic association of birds (and therefore angels) with certain human families is intriguingly demonstrated by the lapwing. A male member of the Lincolnshire family of Tyrwhitts (an old country name for the lapwing, and representative of its haunting, reedy refrain) fell injured in the marshes, and owed his rescue to the persistent alarm-cry of the lapwings, whose unusual behaviour eventually attracted help.

Lapwings seem to like human beings, for they are easily tamed and were once kept as garden birds. Yet their wild, lamenting spirit must never be kept in captivity against their will as they are protected by Bran, one of the noble guardian spirits of Britain. A well-documented incident in folk history tells of a boy living at Colwall in Herefordshire who caught a young lapwing and showed his trophy to the parish clerk's wife. She exhorted him to release it, insisting that if he did not, accident or misfortune would strike him.

The Celtic seer, Fiona Macleod, writes beautifully of the lapwing:

> In the Gaelic imagination the lapwing is something stranger
> and wilder still: a bird of the ancient world, of the
> dispossessed gods, nameless in truth because in truth a god
> nameless and homeless. The Gaelic poet hears in its lament

> the lamentation of what is gone, never to come again,
>   of what long since went away upon the wind, of what
> is going away on the wind: and he has called the *weep*
> [a folk-name for the lapwing] the Birds of the Sorrowful
> Past. Is not the lapwing the bird of Dalua, that unknown
> mysterious god, that terrible shadow who is the invisible,
> inaudible, secret, and dread divinity of weariness, separation,
> gloom, sadness, decay, desolation, madness, despair?

The lapwing is intimately associated with the wellsprings of humanity's darkness and sorrow. Yet I am convinced that it is a saviour bird, allied to the deliverance of the human world from its confusion and suffering.

It is said that those who hated the 'secret', the bright knowledge, hated the gentle lapwing for disguising and protecting it, and in return for her service and self-sacrifice they cast a curse upon her, just as Eve and Mary Magdalene and the true bride of Arthur were outcast and despised and spoken against. And in anciently remote times, Enki, the human 'god' allied to the light of the Divine who fought and laboured valiantly on behalf of humanity against his dark-hearted brother Enlil, employed the wisdom and the magic of the lapwing in order to scupper and scramble his brother's terrible plans, thereby coming to the rescue of beleaguered humanity again and again.

In consideration of all this, my chosen name for the lapwing would be 'the Birds that Sorrow for the past Golden Age' which come to us with their haunting and poignant calls to remind and reawaken us. As if in honour of the lapwing's true calibre, the lapwing is called the Virgin Mary's Dove in Germany, and is welcomed there with delight. And a Muslim legend of the lapwing calls her the Sister of the Brother. The story tells how the lapwing was once a princess who bore a passionate and devoted love for her brother, who had long been absent. One day she heard that he had returned, that he was close at hand and both weary and thirsty. His sister snatched a bowl of hot milk from the fire and ran out to greet him. But an evil-wisher had misinformed her and had hidden away her brother, trusting that the latter would remain undiscovered and his sister would destroy herself in her persistent search. And so it was. The poor sister ran this way and that, calling 'Brother! O Brother!', all the while suffering great pain as the base of the hot bowl of milk that she bore on her head burnt into her crown. For hours, days, even weeks, she searched, until, feeling her strength and her life ebbing away, she called on Allah to help her. And Allah, in his mercy, transformed her into a lapwing so that she could take to the skies and better accomplish her lamenting search.

When Muslim countrywomen hear the cry of the lapwing in the evening, they run from their houses and throw water in the air, that the bird may use it to assuage the pain of the burn on the top of the head, still marked by some black feathers. This horn-like crest inspired the Scottish islanders to call the bird Little Horn of the Rushes, for the lapwing is never far from rushes and reeds in the nesting season.

W B Yeats has said that the wind in the reeds is the whispering voice which speaks to the human soul of the Golden Age long since past … and Enki himself (*see* MERLIN), who could not defy the great parliament of the gods by revealing any part of its discussions and decisions directly to the lesser race of humanity living upon the Earth, spoke instead in the voice of the wind in the reeds, warning the leaders of men of the terrible depredations that his brother Enlil had planned for them so that they might survive. And so the melodious-mouthed lapwing still calls to us, its notes blending with the wind in the reeds, of what might be if we could rise as one and cast off our great sorrow and darkness; and still, when Eastern children look up to see the lapwings circling and crying overhead, they hear in their wheeling, lamenting voices the Arabic words, 'Brother! O Brother!'

This story is similar to the famous African legend of the royal Isis, who went weeping in search of the remains of her beloved brother and husband, Osiris, after he had been murdered and rent apart by his evil brother Seth, and his dismembered body scattered to the four winds.

It echoes, too, the European story of the equally royal Brigid, who walked the world weeping in search of her brother and lover Manannan, lost, dispossessed and frozen in sleep amidst the waste-lands by evil spells. With reference to the female protagonist in each of these key myths, it is interesting to note the Germanic emphasis in

lapwing mythology on the sacred feminine concerning their designation of the bird as the Virgin Mary's Dove. It is indeed the sacrificial
dove of Dalua (the Shadow), perpetually offering itself on his cruel
altar of sorrow and loss to keep safe for us the coming of that day
when his unhallowed pipe can no longer play the music of betrayal
that leads human souls away from the light onto a path of desolate,
benighted wandering.

I had a pair of white doves who tired of living in my garden and
joined a flock of lapwing (the collective noun in the lapwings' case is a
'conceit', denoting the delusionary rather than the arrogant sense of the
word). They lived with them in their main field of habitation all winter
long, taking part in their whirling, circling flight. I received the
impression that these birds of the Holy Spirit had 'run away with the
wild gypsies', and that it was time for my rather too well-ordered
views of spirituality to do the same!

When the lapwing flies into our sphere of being, we must look over
and under, far and near, to uncover the half-glimpsed truths that elude us.

Linnet (see also FINCH)

This sweet-voiced chorister is a fairy bird, most often seen on moorland
and common where the ever-flowering gorse provides thickets of thorns
for its nest. The linnet's song, like a peal of elfin bells, is said to delight
the fairies, who throng in abundance wherever it sings. Their hidden
groves, where they weave their dances, are at once guarded and pro-
claimed by the silvery notes of the linnet. These birds love to sing anthems
to the evening as they give embodiment to the strains of spirit-music emanating from the mystic angel of the twilight and the dying day.

If you hear or see the linnet, however it might fly into your field of
vision, you are being asked to connect again with the wonder and
happiness of childhood, with the world of nature and the innocent
magic of the fairies. They bring the beauty of the ancient soul of nature
to heal and bless you, and to open the eyes of your spirit.

Go out into nature at your next opportunity when you have encountered the linnet, or seek communion with the new or the full Moon, and

contemplate the power and the magic of the fairies as a real influence and source of help in your life.

Magpie

The magpie is said to have a drop of the devil's blood beneath its tongue, and this belief has prompted country people to regard it with respect, chanting rhymes and doffing hats to avert the ill omen when they met it. Esoteric lore regards it as having one foot in the shadow and the other in the light. As such, it represents the human soul, which is attracted by the darkness as well as by the light, and which needs to heal and rescue its shadow-self. The magpie demonstrates this by repeatedly thieving anything that shines. Its dark self craves the light, and, like Prometheus, it constantly steals the divine fire. To see one flying away from the Sun means that the shadow side has triumphed, and the sign is baleful; whilst to see one flying towards the Sun means that it is asserting its radiant side, and the omen is good.

John Clare, the nature poet, had a pet magpie that he taught to imitate human speech. It certainly seemed fascinated by its soul, because it was drawn to its own bright reflection in the waters of a well, which eventually led it to its death by drowning.

The magpie is a bird of prophecy, and gives warning of unhappy events. In the northern midland counties and in Yorkshire, its ominous jabbering rattle is supposed to sound before such mishaps, even if the bird itself is not present at the site of the disaster.

The magpie is so brave in battle, sometimes putting bigger birds to rout, that in cock-fighting days game-fowl eggs were placed for hatching in its nest, in the hope that its fighting spirit would be transferred to its foster chicks.

It is also a bird of balance and stability. Wherever the magpie habitually roosts or perches, be it tree or building, will stand firm against blast or flood and will never be toppled.

When the magpie appears to you, look for the point of balance between the negative and positive forces within yourself. This sacred point is in the heart. Its consciousness is humanity's staunchest anchor.

Its transforming power will overcome all division, all duality, all irreconcilability. When the wound of imbalance or disharmony makes itself known in our lives, only the heart-intelligence can subsume the darkness and heal its suffering. This is the secret of the treasure shining bright in the nest of the magpie.

Mallard (see also DUCK)

The message of the mallard is the same as that for the duck generally, with the additional emphasis that what appears to be tame and domestic can also have its wild side. This augury is good if the element alluded to is liberating, and sinister if it has the potential to oppress.

Mallards have been tamed and domesticated for many centuries, and although they can grow very attached to humans, their emotional nature, so typical of the duck, has caused them to retain the imprint of some of the less desirable traits among humans. A tendency to play fast and loose with their mate, and even to rape, is evident among mallards, although these behaviours do not seem to be typical of other species of duck.

The mallard, still a wild bird despite its long association with domesticity, urges us as a diviner to seek the purity and sanctuary of the wild and to attune to its more sublime aspects. The virgin wilderness calls to the finest aspects of the soul. The other kind of 'wild side' holds a real threat of danger to those who receive the mallard's augury.

Mandarin (see also DUCK)

The overall message of the duck is highlighted in the mandarin's case by colour, elegance and the exotic. These piquant breezes from the realm of the soul will lift you to dizzying heights in your experiences of emotional response. Let them engage the deepest impulses of the heart, and follow the wisdom of the heart, to ensure that you build no castles in the air, or upon the sand, to be laid low by the crashing thunder of the rootless, restless, inappeasable sea, or the undifferentiated ferocity of emotionalism.

The wise mandarin whistles: 'Embrace faith, courage, and self-giving; eschew seduction!'

Martin (House)

The martin is considered to be a token from the heaven-worlds, affirming the presence of the Divine Spirit and bringing luck and happiness to humankind. It is a bird of summer, of our true home beyond the veil, and brings the touch of the Goddess to each house where it chooses to roost.

'The martin and the swallow', says an old saw, 'are God's mate and marrow'. Occasionally the last line of the rhyme differs; variants are 'God's bow and arrow' or 'God Almighty's birds to hallow', but the meaning is the same – birds sent from heaven. When the martin comes to you, it bids you rise up to heaven with it, even whilst you live your life on Earth.

It cries: 'Spread the wings of your spirit and come with me to the eternal summerlands. You are always welcome, you can gain admittance at any time – just believe, just follow me!'

Martin (Sand) *(see also* MARTIN (HOUSE)) *(N. America:* **Bank Swallow)**

The augury of this bird, taken in conjunction with that of the house martin, tells of soul reflection and quiet contemplation. It is one of the birds that urge us to take up the practice of meditation.

It flies over expanses of inland waters, and nests in sandy banks. It reminds us that our dwelling-place of the physical body upon the Earth is indeed a house built on sand, fragile, subject to shifts of the tide, and ultimately perishable.

Its message is not so ecstatic as that of the house martin, which bids us seek bliss. The sand martin, less of an arrow in its anatomical shape, encourages us to seek the clear, still waters of the soul, and reflect serenely upon our greater being. It calls to us to seek depth.

Merganser (Red-Breasted) *(see also* DUCK)

This bird brings the same augury as other ducks, pointing particularly to the balancing of the emotions involving domesticity and home and those which belong to wider, more far-ranging issues. With its wispy crest it signifies ever-roaming, gypsy royalty.

Merlin (see also HAWK)

This small lady's hawk is said to be a mysterious, elfin bird. As the smallest falcon, it shares a magical relationship with the eagle, the largest bird of prey. This link between the hawk and the eagle is highlighted in the ancient tale of 'The Hawk of Achill', commonly supposed to be a merlin, which belongs to the sacred story-cycles of the Celtic bards of the druidic brotherhood.

> The story tells how the hawk of Achill was present in the newest dawn of a new epoch, when one Beltane Eve (30 April, also known as Walpurgis Night, at which time spirits leave their realm to walk and wander in the mortal world) a terrible cold fell and locked the Earth in thrall. Nothing so severe was ever experienced again, until one night it revisited the world so that everything froze under its spell.
>
> To save itself, the hawk of Achill flew to shelter in an eagle's nest, killing and removing the solitary fledgling it found there. When the she-eagle returned, she noticed no difference and fed the hawk as if it were her own young. As she brooded over the hawk, she remarked that never could there have been such a cruelly cold night as the present one. The hawk replied that one had indeed occurred, countless years ago, which was even more extreme in its severity. When the she-eagle questioned the hawk as to how it could remember such an event when it was only just a month old, the hawk advised her to ask the blackbird at the forge, so old that he had worn a thick iron bar almost in two by repeatedly cleaning his beak on it, to verify the story.
>
> 'I am too young to remember,' said the blackbird. 'Ask the stag, who has lived for more than four thousand years,

and whose cast antlers have furnished sufficient fencing to surround a one-acre field.' The stag declared that he also was too young to recollect the event, but that she must ask the blind salmon of Assaroe, who was even older than he.

The salmon told the eagle that there had indeed come a night, many thousands of years ago, when he had been frozen as if by enchantment into the ice of his sacred pool, and the hawk of Achill had flown down and pecked out his eyes, which was why he was blind to this day. The salmon further informed the eagle that he suspected that she had unwittingly been harbouring the Hawk of Achill in her nest. The eagle returned in a fury at dawn to find her nest empty and the hawk gone.

This is a compelling story, with such recognizable features that it is worth dwelling on. It seems to be a myth that enshrines the promise of ascension embodied in the mystery of the Holy Grail. For a full examination of the links between this ancient folk tale, the history of the Emerald Tablet and the Holy Grail, please *see* Appendix 1.

By the magical deeds of the arch-druid Merlin – the merlin, smallest and yet, in magical terms, greatest of the hawks – the ancestral knowledge, that knowledge which emerges from the source of spirit within us all, will rise again and transform human consciousness. The Grail will be restored to the Earth, as the deepest, most sacred esoteric secrets attest. That is why the merlin sent the eagle to those creatures symbolizing the secrets of the unbeguiled masculine principle – the Fishman, the noble stag, and the male blackbird – called the 'merle' in Celtic tradition. When the eagle returns to find her nest empty, the sacred story tells us that the cycle is broken and transformation has already begun. When the merlin draws close, the augury is momentous.

In the legends of King Arthur, Galahad is the pure knight who at last attains the Grail. He is, of course, taken straight up to heaven. He has not died, but has achieved ascension – the state of heaven – whilst still on Earth. This is the promise and the gift of the Holy Grail. And in the Celtic language of Wales, Galahad was called

Gwalch-y-Had – the Hawk of Summer – the solar hawk – the merlin. Ascension is assured.

Moorhen

These lovely little birds of quiet inland waters are the fowl of small things; little events, little challenges, small kindnesses, little blessings, little sorrows, little trials, small failings, humble accomplishments and masteries; the diminutive stitches that knit together a life.

The soft lilting warble of the moorhen sounding over the dark expanse of the dullest ditch gives to the waters a sweet hallowed magic, a twinkle of mystery, revealing that even these mundane backwaters are the stuff of the soul and can reflect the stars; profound depths are miraculously present even in the shallow muddy ditch.

The moorhen says: 'There is smallness – but there need not be pettiness; there is humbleness – but there need not be triviality. The wind of the spirit speaks not less sweetly to the blade of grass than to the mightiest tree of the forest.'

Nightingale

This exquisite bird of love's delight and sorrow sings sweetly throughout both day and night, despite its name. Its lyrical name is 'philomel', meaning love of song or melody, taken from the Greek legend whereby the gods prevented the Thracian king from slaying the two daughters of an Athenian king, one of whom he had ravished and one of whom was his wife. The gods transformed the two sisters, Philomela and Procne, into a nightingale and a swallow, whilst their would-be murderer was changed into a hoopoe. Because Philomela had suffered the loss of her tongue at the Thracian king's hands, the compensating gods gave her poetic justice by bestowing on her the rapturous song of the nightingale, whilst Procne, who had lost the summer of her years, was given the distinction of becoming the bird that eternally brings the summer.

Folklore says that the nightingale produces its beautiful song by singing with its breast pressing against a thorn, inducing a melody of such sweetness that the poet Keats thought of it as a spirit and wrote, 'Thou wast not born for death, immortal bird...'

When the nightingale appears in your life, she comes to remind you of the two aspects of love, its sweetness and its sorrow, because only thus can love's two arms reach around the rim of the world and melt the icy ignorance which locks the heart of humanity. The nightingale's song is said to be magical, an angel's song, and to open worlds of enchantment to the listener.

Nightjar (see also HAWK and MERLIN)

This night hawk is an ally of the merlin in that it comes to teach us about higher consciousness and to lead us towards ascension. We must enter the night, the stills, the deeps of the worlds that lie within us in order to ascend in consciousness. We must swoop down upon and hold and claim the creatures of enlightenment which are meant to fuse with us and nourish us. Then, when the merlin's prophecy is fulfilled and the Holy Grail returns to the Earth, we will be able to avail ourselves of it without encumbrance.

The nightjar is a bird that guides us towards the practice of meditation as an essential in our lives. It has a very particular augural function in that it alerts us to the possibility that we may not be using sufficient discipline whilst meditating, but tending to drift off and amble happily amongst pleasant images instead of challenging the superficiality in ourselves and aiming deeper, higher, to attain a more sublime level of perception, a greater profundity of vision.

Just as Tibetan monks in training receive a sharp slap on the top of the head, applied by their teacher from time to time during meditation, to ensure that they are not merely taking a nap, so the nightjar claps its wings together over its back, making a distinct slapping sound, during its display flights!

The nightjar feeds on aerial rather than terrestrial prey, emphasizing its connection to winged consciousness. It comes to inspire us and to urge us to greater breakthroughs in our lives. Its soft call cries to us: 'Seek the wonders of the abysm within!'

Nuthatch

The attractive, eccentric little nuthatch with its upper plumage of soft blue-grey teaches us to be mindful of our happiness. Foresight, clear-seeing, perceptive philosophy, common sense and intelligence need to be applied to the way we live our lives, or we may mistake a brick wall for the way forward!

The song of the nuthatch is rich and varied, of surprising volume, interspersed with whistling notes up and down the scale as if it sings to us to look at things from every angle and to take the broader, grander, comprehensive view.

It loves deciduous woods, emphasizing the seasons of life, of relationships, of every enterprise or journey (for dawn, morning, noon, afternoon, evening, sunset and the close of night are all seasons).

It alone among British bird species travels down tree-trunks head first, like a little torpedo! With its loud, off-beat song it calls to us to dare to see things in an unconventional light, and urges: 'Look where you are going! Head-first, not feet-first!'

Oriole (Golden)

In magical lore, the beautiful golden oriole is hailed as a transfigured mirror-image of the blackbird. We know from blackbird lore (*see* BLACKBIRD, *and also* MERLIN) that the blackbird is associated with the very core of our being. It is linked with our ancestral and spiritual source and with the sacred smith of the world, who is the God-inspired dynamic of our collective and individual soul as through elemental alchemy we forge ourselves into being in the sphere of materiality, whose symbol is the hallowed, but somewhat hellish, blacksmith's forge.

The golden oriole is the aura of light forming the mystic circle of creation whose centre is the black dot, the blackbird. The blackbird is the pupil of the eye and the golden oriole the light of the Divine streaming through it to create consciousness. When the magical smith within us all has completed his-her great work, we will find that the blackbird has become the golden oriole, and yet still remains the shining darkness, the unspoken mystery in which all is contained. And so the mirror of the spirit reflects the blackbird reflecting the golden oriole, and their merged symbolism is another symbol of ascension, of humanity brought to perfection, and of the Holy Grail.

As we might expect of such a bird, the golden oriole is secretive and spends much of its time aloft in the treetops. It has a special affinity with the poplar, and loves to nest in this tree above all others. The poplar is known as the 'whispering tree' because of its rustling, ever-dancing leaves which are set quivering by the slightest breath of wind. Folklore celebrates the poplar as the tree with the most acute hearing, a 'listening' tree as well as a 'whispering' tree. The golden oriole is said to be attuned to this soul-sensitivity of inner listening. Its love of the poplar is interesting, because the tree is dedicated to Persephone, the goddess of darkness and light who spends six months of darkness in the underworld and six radiant months above ground in the golden sunshine of the spring and summer months. Golden crowns of poplar leaves discovered in the royal burial mounds of ancient Sumer (the civilization of antiquity which had knowledge of the Emerald Tablet) also emphasize the poplar's link with the spiritual aspect of gold and goldenness.

When the golden oriole comes to you, it is showing you that the magical smith within is ready to work his divine alchemy and reflect the wonder of the golden oriole through some transformation in your life – a transformation born from the secrets that the darkness in your life has revealed to you. It will show you that secreted in the darkness are seeds of light ready to yield a golden harvest.

Both the blackbird and the golden oriole have whistling songs – they are pipers of the dawn and of the soft shades of evening. The flute-like calls of the golden oriole say: 'Listen, listen, listen to the winds of the spirit, and you will learn how to infuse your world with gold!'

Osprey (see also HAWK)

Known as the fisher hawk, this bird of prey, according to traditional lore, loves to build its nest in some darkly evocative and romantic setting, such as a storm-blasted tree or a solitary ruined tower. J B Rittenhouse says of it in his *A Bird Lover's Anthology*:

> On a gaunt and shattered tree
>
> By the black cliffs of obsidian
>
> I saw the nest of the osprey.
>
> Nothing remained of the tree
>
> For this lonely eyrie
>
> Save the undaunted bole.

Lewis Dunbar, a Victorian professional egg-collector who contributed to the demise of the osprey in Britain, (it now enjoys protected sites for breeding and is making a recovery) recorded one such traditional breeding site in his description of an eyrie built on top of a tower belonging to a ruined castle on Loch Eilein. The lore of the osprey seems to recognize that its magical significance should be announced via a wild, lonely, evocative setting that speaks of sorrow, grandeur and poignant beauty, as of a wonder lost and yet hauntingly, pensively present.

The magnificent spectacle of the osprey as it dives with impressive legs and talons outstretched into inland waters, grasps a fish, scatters a riot of diamond drops as it vigorously shakes dry its plumage and then rises dramatically to the heavens with its prize in a swirl of white spray, is a stirring sight.

It is no wonder that this bird too is associated with the mysterious and majestically remote Fisher King (*see* KINGFISHER), and that folklore deems the bird a fisher of souls. Like the Fisher King, the osprey has been persecuted mercilessly throughout its territories. The Fisher King was said to signify the bereaved union of the spiritual masculine and the spiritual feminine principles, and in fact we find that in folklore the osprey is reputed to have one taloned foot for hunting and one goose's foot for swimming and treading water (the goose is an archetypal matriarchal symbol).

The osprey comes to us to sound the declaration that victory will prevail. If you have devoted yourself to what may seem a lost cause, if you need courage to continue on a path that you believe is right, despite discouragement from others or even persecution, the osprey is your ally.

It seemed to hit its mark so many times on its hunting expeditions that it was believed to have a special power of enchantment over its quarry. The poet George Peel, writing in 1594, described this folk belief:

> I will provide thee of a princely osprey,
>
> That, as he flieth over fish in pools,
>
> The fish shall turn their glistering bellies up
>
> And thou shalt take thy liberal choice of all.

This idea of the osprey as a master hunter, wielding a magician-like quality in its ability to achieve its aims, was precisely what caused it to be so ruthlessly persecuted. It teaches us that we should never allow envy, ignorance and spite to undermine our aspirations and our self-belief. The strange, wild, high-pitched mew of the osprey cries: 'Ignore adversity! Triumph shall be yours!'

Ostrich

The augury of the ostrich is not quite what it might at first appear. It is true that this huge, landlocked bird buries its head in the sand or in a bush, imagining thereby that it is hidden from its pursuers because it cannot itself see them; but this act of apparent stupidity is not straightforward.

The gaze of the ostrich is reputed to be powerfully magical. It was believed that the bird hatched its eggs by gazing profoundly and steadfastly upon them, and that if her visual focus was distracted for even a moment, the eggs became addled. The mother ostrich, in her wisdom, knew if one of her eggs was bad, and would remove and destroy it. A verse from Southey conforms to this belief:

> Oh! even with such a look, as fables say
>
> The mother ostrich fixes on her eggs,
>
> Till that intense affection
>
> Kindle its light of life.

It was the habit of several Eastern Churches to suspend ostrich eggs near the altar as a tutelary symbol of God's watchful care. The eye of God was seen as functioning in the same way as the eye of the ostrich, and even to look through it as an expression of the Divine presence.

The supernatural gaze of the ostrich with its magical virtues of incubation, the bestowal of life and the power of discernment between good and evil was considered almost Buddha-like in its ability to pronounce on the illusory and the real. It might even be supposed that if the ostrich removed its pursuers from its field of vision and gazed hard enough on their subsequent absence, perhaps the power of its vision would truly spirit them out of existence!

The stomach of the ostrich is also remarkable. It can digest almost anything, and in fact the ostrich swallows large stones to aid the function of its gizzard. When it is confined where it cannot obtain them, it will swallow pieces of iron, copper, brick, or even glass.

When the ostrich presents itself to you, it points to tremendous strengths, remarkable abilities, which distinguish you from the crowd and make you special. You might be able to 'stomach' all kinds of challenging situations. Within the context of this specialness, it is important not to use your abilities tritely, or to imagine that because you possess them you are of greater importance, or more protected and favoured, than anyone else. This complacency would lead you into difficulties. However potent her gaze, the ostrich does not usually throw off her pursuers by burying her head in the sand!

The ostrich asks you to recognize that indeed you do have gifts beyond the average reach, and that they must be properly honoured and set in their right context. Out of context, they will be of no help to you, and might even prove a hindrance. The ostrich advises: 'Do not allow your extraordinary strengths to become a dangerous source of weakness!' (We could with justification, for instance, imagine that the ostrich might have made itself known to Mrs Thatcher in the latter years of her term of office!)

Ouzel (Ring) (*see also* BLACKBIRD)

The ring ouzel is of similar size and plumage to the blackbird, and as sweet a chorister (although its song is more similar to that of the thrush). The great difference between the two is that the ouzel wears a 'crescent moon' of white feathers around its throat. This 'moonlight' extends to its wing feathers, causing them to appear a soft silver-grey in flight.

If the blackbird is the winged, melodious creature of the sacred darkness, the ring ouzel is the bird of the night's eye – the glimpsing eye of the sickle moon. It shows us that our inner eye is beginning to open onto the exquisite worlds of light that dwell in the womb that is the sacred darkness. The crescent moon around the throat – a great centre of the life-forces and the transformer of these life-forces into the rapturous song of the ouzel, which is a promise that we will sound forth the new harmonies of the worlds of light we are discovering – shows us both the eye within ourselves that is opening, and the virgin, pearly light of the newly-encountered spheres.

We may draw from the augury of the ouzel that we are on the verge of some deeply significant understanding. It may be that we begin to see at last where the darkness has brought us and what beautiful transfigurations it has wrought, smith-like, within us (which is the work of the indwelling blacksmith, the smith of the sacred darkness). It may be that we are ready for spiritual unfoldment, or that we begin to see something or someone in a new, inspired light. 'You will pass into higher vision!' promises the mellifluent song of the ring ouzel.

This bird is a fierce defender of its young, which in its augural sense means that its protective spirit watches over the newly-born vision that is stirring within its sphere of guardianship. You are promised a protector, a custodian from the spiritual spheres, as your awakening gathers pace.

Owl

In old Welsh the word for 'owl' is *blodeuwedd*, the name of a magical woman-of flowers who was created for the purpose of providing a wife for Lleu, a Sun-deity. Restless as his escort, Blodeuwedd asserted her independence and left Lleu. As punishment, the enchanter Gwydion turned her into an owl, doomed to be despised by all other birds and so only able to come out at night.

This unhappy myth of the owl seems to correspond with the time when the Celtic goddesses were suddenly denounced and the ascendancy of male deities ensured that the Celtic priestesses were divested of their authority and regarded as witches, who just like the owl were despised by their communities and said to come out at night.

In fact the beautiful and fascinating owl species has abilities and peculiarities that belong to no other bird, and has always been associated with the feminine powers of the soul. Rather than being a bird of death and ill-omen, it is an escorter of the spirit to the otherworldly realms. Whenever a death occurred in the Wardour family of Arundel, two large white owls appeared on the house-roof shortly before the event, and throughout folk-history similar tales have been reported.

The owl is sacred to Athene, Greek goddess of wisdom, to Minerva, Roman goddess of handicrafts, learning and war, and to Diana, divine huntress of the night. As well as Diana, the owl is associated with many of the Moon goddesses and a number of the Celtic star-goddesses. The owl is also sacred to the Olympian god of healing, Asclepius, and owl eggs, feathers and meat were used in many folk remedies. They provided particular protection from the frenzies and the furies at every level of life.

In esoteric lore the owl is a symbol of wisdom, silence, meditation, night and all hidden things, and also of victory in battle. 'I rejoice that there are owls,' said the 19th-century American writer, Henry Thoreau. 'Wise midnight hags! They represent the stark twilight and unsatisfied thoughts we all have.' He thought that their cries 'suggested a vast and undeveloped nature which men have not recognized'. It might be that he was receiving intimations of the twilit landscapes of the sacred feminine, denied and kept in darkness and lamented over by the owl's cry. Perhaps this accounts for the tradition that if a man looks into an owl's nest (its secret place of power and symbol of its origin) he will be melancholy all his life. An ancient verse from the songs of the Celtic Bards concerning the owl reads:

> I am coeval with the ancient oak
>
> Whose roots spread wide in yonder moss,
>
> Many a race has passed before me,
>
> And still I am the lonely owl of Srona.

What the owl seeks to reveal has still not been recognized in the psyche of humankind, in spite of the long history it has endured and the civilizations it has seen come and go. The owl signifies the senses of the soul – what the greater soul sees, hears, embraces, scents and savours. Until this higher consciousness is recognized by the earthly mind, the owl is destined to be alone, and to utter songs of loneliness in the solitude of the night as she waits, ever waits, for the dawn and for her essence, made of flowers, to come into its own once more.

The owl is particularly linked with ivy as well as to the famous oak. Ivy, in addition to the oak, is a 'tree' sacred to the Druids. It is a symbol of Saturn the tester, of the hourglass of time and of primal darkness; but it is also a plant associated with conjugal love, with healing, and with protection from storms and evil spells. It is a feminine plant expressing the principle of the sacred number three or the pyramid, which is itself a symbol of feminine wisdom. The ivy is shunned and feared in folklore precisely because of its connection with this forbidden wisdom; and the ancientness of the Goddess and her hidden knowledge is often conceptually degraded into the image of the horrific night-hag. This is the root of the ignorance which shuns the owl, the bird which can turn its head, its consciousness, full circle and so perceive life in its entirety.

When the owl appears to you, it alerts you to your own powers of clairvoyance, to the purified senses of the higher soul, and brings you a message concerning wise detachment, discernment and clear-seeing. It asks you to nurture your vision of the higher worlds by the art of meditation, perhaps walking meditations in the twilight amongst nature, as well as the more usual methods. It reminds you that it is a bird of change, initiation and new beginnings, and heralds triumph in your struggles. As a bird of the Goddess, it represents birth and death; but the true interpretation of death is that when something in our lives comes to an end, a new birth takes place, and a hidden door opens.

Oystercatcher

The oystercatcher, with its vivid black-and-white plumage and its fiery orange beak, legs and claws, is traditionally the bird sacred to Brigid, who was the supreme goddess of the north long before she became Christianized as St Bride. Brigid was a triple goddess and, interestingly, we find a St Bridget spoken of in folklore who was said to have been born in England, Scotland and Ireland, and who was also known in Wales, Cornwall and the Isle of Man. Bishop Cormac, in his *Glossary*, cited Brigid as: 'A goddess whom the bards [Druids] worshipped, for very great and noble was her perfection. Her sisters [aspects] were Brigid, the Woman of Healing, and Brigid, the Smith-Woman.' The third and central aspect of Brigid was the Woman of Compassion. She was the embodiment of wisdom, and the oystercatcher, which feeds on shellfish, has been observed breaking open oysters and revealing the treasure of their indwelling pearls (*see* Appendix 3).

The pearl, a lunar jewel, has from time immemorial been associated with wisdom, creation, and the Goddess. The pearl is pure white, except that it contains an infinitesimal point of black in its composition. The black point or dot is the sacred darkness from which all divine light issues. Scientists tell us that once the entire universe was a black dot, which began to expand and become as it is today (it is still expanding). The oystercatcher's black and white plumage attests to this mystery of the divine light and the sacred darkness; its flame-hued bill, legs and claws intimate Brigid's holy fire. Fiona Macleod says of this bird:

> Fisher-folk on the shores of the west and on the far isles
> have gladdened at the first prolonged repetitive whistle of
> the oyster-opener, for its advent means that the hosts of
> the good fish are moving towards the welcoming coasts
> once more, that the wind of the south is unloosened, that
> greenness will creep to the grass, that birds will seek the
> bushes, that song will come to them, and that everywhere
> a new gladness will be abroad.

The oystercatcher sometimes masses in flocks thousands strong. In the Scottish isles they are called the 'clans of the pipers', because this live-wire bird, with occasionally as many as 30 companions, runs along the ground piping volubly in order to establish a territory.

When the oystercatcher reveals itself, the tender Brigid, purest and greatest of goddesses, is drawing close to you. Her augury is of healing, of compassion, of the bestowing of pearls of wisdom, of the work of the she-smith within each one of us, regardless of gender. Brigid also brings protection. The sign of the oystercatcher foretells that you will receive these gifts in rich abundance.

Parakeet (Ring-Necked)

The parakeet established itself in the southeast of Britain and in other parts of northwest Europe in the middle of the 20th century, although it is properly native to India and Africa, where it populates jungles and areas of human civilization.

Its augury is one of love, or of some other unexpected and exotic experience swooping suddenly into our lives. It especially emphasizes healing via the experience of love, whether through sorrow or joy. Usually, though, the parakeet promises a happy love affair. It comes to tell you that an unsuspected source of love, not invariably of a romantic nature, is soon to be released from your deepest being, which in itself will be a healing force for you and for others. Healing through the release of beautiful and inspiring emotion, of a kind that calls forth happy and creative visions of future possibilities that can be realized through the application of will, intuitive guidance and the radiant dynamic of love, is the parakeet's prognostication.

Parrot

The parrot is a wise old bird. It is said that parrots can attain the age of 300 years, which, significantly, is the mythological age-span of the eagle. They certainly live considerably longer than human beings, due to their resistance to oxidizing elements in the air. Because of this unique resilience or 'wisdom' of its breathing-cycles, the parrot is considered sacred by the indigenous peoples of its countries of origin.

The parrot's gaze is as penetrating and majestic as that of the eagle, challenging our mental and emotional attachment to narrowness and littleness. The parrot clambers more than it flies. It has a well-documented sense of humour and a strong sense of its own dignity. When it learns to imitate human speech, it does not simply reproduce the words with mechanical efficiency, but catches every nuance, every subtle sound-pattern, in the voice of the imitated. It thereby crafts a mirror in which we can observe how we present ourselves to the world. Looking into it through the medium of sound, we can gain insight and revelations that would not otherwise be possible, and begin to challenge and overturn our limitations.

The parrot initiates potential wise men and wise women among tribal peoples into the office of shaman. In South America the process is described thus:

> The future shaman walks in the forest and suddenly sees a
> bird perch within reach of his hand, then vanish. Flocks of
> parrots fly down toward him and disappear as if by magic.
> The future shaman goes home shaking and uttering
> unintelligible words. An odour of decay and annatto
> emanates from his body (he has died to his old, uninitiated
> self). Suddenly a gust of wind makes him totter; he falls like
> a dead man. At this moment he has become the receptacle
> of a spirit that speaks through his mouth. From now on he
> is a shaman.

A Métraux, *Le Shamanisme chez les Indiens de l'Amérique
du Sud Tropicale*

Looking at life with a quizzical eye, the parrot comes to remind us of our birthright, our heritage, our innate royalty. Human beings have been given a divine gift unlike any other. The parrot would have us ponder on this, and urges us to remember further that we are not on Earth for any ignoble or mundane purpose. If we have lost touch with our magical, inspired, spiritually journeying self, the parrot advises that we return to source and look to our breath, for the breath is indeed magical. We breathe in the holiness of our source with every breath we take; each out-breath can be an expression of our divinity. The breath is our connection to the ineffable. Take a few minutes each day to sit and breathe easily, a little more slowly than usual, in complete breath-cycles, with a brief and comfortable pause between each one. Breathe in whatever you need – strength, endurance, peace, healing, a break-through in understanding – all is there at your divine source, and its ever-replenished reserves can be drawn on in abundance through the magical act of breathing.

The parrot, with its deafening squawk, rudely awakens us out of our sleep of complacency and spiritual idleness, and urges us to aim for higher things. It announces: 'Take the long, broad, grand highway as far as your perspective is concerned, because life is eternal! You are eternal! You are the shaman of your own soul.'

Partridge

It is said that this bird tells of ardour and warns of jealousy. Perdix ('partridge') was a Greek Sun deity, nephew and pupil of Daedalus, who was an inventor. His uncle was arrogant concerning his achieve-ments and could not tolerate the idea of a rival. After producing some ingenious inventions by imitating nature, among them the compass and the saw, Perdix roused the wrath of Daedalus, who cast his nephew off a high tower.

Minerva, goddess of handicrafts, saw him falling and, anxious to save a favourite, transformed Perdix into a partridge.

Since then, the partridge is careful not to nest in trees, shuns high places and in flight it never lifts itself far above the ground. It is a bird sacred to the Sun, to fertility and sexuality, associated with goddesses of love and carnal passion. The hen is said to be so sensitively attuned to the principle of consummation and abundance that she can be impreg-nated by the sound of the cock's voice, or his scent on the wind.

When the partridge comes as messenger, it speaks of the goodness of the physical earth and her fecundity, of the warm blessings of a harmonious family life, of the sweetness of corporeal life, perhaps of a love affair that is about to blossom. It also reminds us how we need to protect love, from our own jealousy and destructive thoughts and actions, and those of others.

Partridge (Common, English or Grey)
(*see also* PARTRIDGE)

The grey partridge bears the general augury of the partridge, with the difference that it encourages us to be less reticent concerning our skills, talents and gifts. We are urged not to hide our light under a bushel. Neither should we doubt our own attractiveness, our personal magnetism. When we can overcome this tendency, the warm, rich promises of the partridge can come into being in our lives.

Partridge (Red-Legged) (*see also* PARTRIDGE)

The auspice given for the partridge belongs in full to this bird, plus a single warning note. Be careful of a rival, and that this rival does not interfere with your rightful claim to the happiness that the partridge prophesies. It counsels that the best way to deal with a rival is to avoid direct confrontation or challenge. Throw a garment of psychic invisibility around your actions and intentions, and play your cards from under the table.

Its rattling, chuckling call says: 'You will know when it is time to display, when it is time to show your hand.'

Peacock

This bird is associated with the queen of heaven and with royalty. In Greece, the bird was sacred to Hera, the ruling goddess, and in Rome to Juno, 'first among goddesses'. The 'eyes' on its feathers represent the all-seeing eye of the Godhead, or the eye of Horus, the single-eyed hawk-son of Isis and Osiris who fought the evil Seth in the name of his father, the Sun god. Later belief attributed the decoration on the peacock's tail to the 'evil eye', and so the feathers were considered unlucky.

When this bird presents itself to you, it brings a royal endorsement, and encouragement to take pride in yourself and your endeavours: that pride which is true pride and gives a quiet dignity and stability to a life rather than the foolishness of conceit, which has the opposite effect.

Pelican

Beautifully portrayed in many ancient stained-glass church windows, the pelican is a symbol of charity. St Heironymous related a story of a pelican restoring its young to life after they had been destroyed by serpents. It resurrected them with its own blood, thereby making the pelican an emblem of Christ. An even older story from Physiologus tells how pelicans are model parents, but that, as the chicks grow older, they rebel against the male until he turns on them and kills them. After three days, the mother bird returns to the nest where the dead nestlings lie, broods them and, piercing her breast, pours blood on them, whereby they are miraculously restored to life, afterwards feeding them on her breast-blood until they attain maturity.

In fact, during its breeding season the pelican macerates the fish it catches in a large pouch under its bill. To feed its young it catches this bag by pressing it against its breast, and then transfers the contents of the pouch to the mouths of its young. Because of the length and sharpness of the pelican's great beak, it seems that this can sometimes result in bleeding.

The unusual habits of the pelican and their symbolism have ensured that it has been regarded as a sacred and shamanic bird since time immemorial, and its augury echoes this age-old wisdom. Some project or relationship, involving the chance to materialize your deepest dream, will shortly become available to you. You have the resources to usher it into being, but bringing it to full fruition will involve sacrifice of the highest order – as it were, your own heart's blood. If you can countenance such a great act of giving forth, of overflowing charity (which is a decision you should make without outside pressure), then a wonderful spiritual renewal, a surging forth of the divine life-forces, will surely follow.

To help you in your mission, the pelican's cry asks you to repeat its motto: 'I Am the Resurrection and the Life!' as an affirmation, the 'I Am' referring to the divine spark or spirit, God, within us all.

Penguin

Whereas the puffin is the clown of the rocky colonies, the penguin is the institutional grand old gentleman. Its name derives from the Welsh *pen* (head), and *Gwyn* or *Gwion*, the original name of Taliesin, Radiant-Brow, he of the Bright Knowledge. Taliesin, the supreme Welsh bard, is closely linked with Enki (*see* LAPWING *and* IBIS). Many motifs reveal him as Enki's spiritual son. We may read in *pen-gwion*, then, the secret that this bird is a symbol of the origins and the highest principles – the fountain-head – of the Bright Knowledge. It is interesting to think, in this context, of the Penguin series of scholarly, high-brow publications!

Although its walk and its general mien are comical, even more outwardly so than the puffin's, its essence is of stalwart, rock-solid fundamentals. It represents the basic principles upon which life is founded. Although these may appear to adhere to the common perception of the law of the jungle or Darwinian survival of the fittest, the penguin knows better. The principles of life are civilizing and judicious, and the penguin, in its Victorian black coat and its Templar and Masonic black-and-white, espouses these 'gentle' values. Although it experiences the harshest conditions on the planet, it masses together in large groups to retain its integrity and outfaces the very worst that ethical snow and ice and unrelenting winter can do to undermine its moral certitude. It is a symbol of good conscience, of the enlightened, all-wise intuition.

From the spiritual standpoint, its muttering, geriatric, ancient wisdom-keeping call chunters: 'The rocks remain!' When the penguin makes itself known to you, its message may be a complex one, involving all of the detail given above; or it may be simple and direct, such as 'Back to basics!'

Peregrine Falcon (see also HAWK)

This is the king's falcon. It represents the hawk's symbolism and essence at its most exalted. When this bird comes to you, you have won favour with the gods, and are urged to behave within the dictates of your highest nature.

Petrel (Leach's)

Leach's petrel is a mysterious bird of romantic associations, living out on the wild ocean for most of the year, and approaching breeding sites on land only at night. It is a night visitor, too, to ships sailing the high seas, and sailors look out for these nocturnal 'swallows' as they follow their vessel under the stars.

They are birds of happy omen, foretelling the release of good, creative energy, perhaps by an initial clearing of negative or blocked energy; perhaps by an output of adventurous, industrious effort, or by some unexpected opportunity presenting itself. Whatever it is, you will achieve victory, and it will be as if miracles are wrought in your life.

The petrel's musical cry exclaims: 'Ride the winds, let the strength of the spirit bear you up, and you will achieve mastery and joy!'

Petrel (Storm) (see also PETREL (LEACH'S))

The augury is the same as for Leach's petrel, except that in the case of the storm petrel the prophecy foretells that a crisis or a confrontation may serve to clear the air. The birds were known as 'Mother Carey's Chickens', the friends of sailors as they came to warn them of impending storms, and drowned seamen were reputed to speak and prophesy through their cries.

The storm petrel reminds us that although there is grandeur, beauty and evocative wildness that awakens the soul in the drama of the great storms that break over land and sea, and although we may perceive shining peaks of power and majestic movement in their momentum which the soul longs to command, the emotional and cerebral storms that conflagrate in human life do not belong to the same pure spirit as the angelic forces that meet and consummate in the upper airs of the natural world. Our human storms need to be soothed and brought under control, because their mighty elemental forces, expressing themselves through a human medium, can only become ugly, destructive and draining and lead us off course.

The storm petrel, which is the spirit of storm-wisdom, advises us that when our human storms arise and the first release is over, it is wise to command the raging elemental forces and calm and contain them until their jangling vibrations are soothed. The storm petrel will show us how to do this without surrendering our own power to domination by others. Its purring message is: 'Blessed are the peacemakers!'

Phalarope

The phalarope signifies the heart of friendship. Although it is a bird of the wild seas, wintering in the Atlantic Ocean, it is paradoxically a bird of prepossessingly tame habits which seems actively to like having humans around.

It embraces polar opposites, and is happy with its spiritual identity as a bird of contrasts. Expect unusual friendships to proffer themselves, with animals and with facets of the natural world as well as with other people, when the warm-coloured summer-plumaged phalarope makes itself known to you. If it appears to you in its sombre winter garb, it is asking you to set aside more time and effort, to be more giving, within the context of your existing friendships, and to take care that you are not blind to arising opportunities to forge new ones. Sometimes it suggests that you are being actively unfriendly, perhaps to the environment or to a colleague or even to yourself. Whatever it is that is dulling your life-experience through wrong relationship, the friendly phalarope will give you its spiritual inspiration to put things right.

Pheasant

Not properly native to Europe, although now long established, the pheasant arrived on British shores at about the same time as the disciples began to establish Christianity on the island, which seems to have been much earlier than orthodox history records (*see The Lost Disciples*, George F Jowett). The Romans introduced it as a table bird (they also introduced rabbits as a similar delicacy). The pheasant originally hailed from south-east Russia and Asia, and in fact its name derives from *Phasis*, a river south of the Caucasus running into the Black Sea, in which area the bird had established natural and extensive breeding grounds. The Greek name of the river *Phasis* has now changed to *Rion*, but its heritage lives on in the name of this royal bird.

The theft of a pheasant's egg carried the penalty of a year's imprisonment under Henry VIII, and although it does not now enjoy the same status as the swan, the royal prerogative was certainly once similarly associated with the pheasant. Crested birds were always linked with the concept of monarchy, and the pheasant's crest is a particularly fine and striking purple, the colour of royalty.

Alexander Pope waxed sorrowfully lyrical over this majestic and remorselessly hunted bird in a verse from 'Windsor Forest':

> Ah! what avail his glossy, varying dyes,
>
> His purple crest, and scarlet-circled eyes,
>
> The vivid green his shining plumes unfold,
>
> His painted wings, and breast that flames with gold?

Although the cock pheasant enjoys a multiplicity of wives and is said to ignore them after fertilizing their eggs, I have observed much less cavalier behaviour in my own pheasant friends. A devoted couple, cock and hen, walked the length of the lane running beside my house together without fail every spring and summer night for several years, even though there was no scarcity of hen pheasants, should the cock have chosen to establish a harem. His considerable size also confirmed that he was no juvenile. Visitors to my cottage were greatly amused to see them taking their 'evening constitutional' together! Nevertheless, a monarchic attitude to fidelity does seem to prevail generally amongst the strutting cock pheasant, which is often a solitary bird, with a certain ring of pathos in its strident, clamorous, yet strangely musical call.

One of the most intriguing aspects concerning the pheasant is its connection with the mythological Chinese Feng bird and the phoenix, and in fact the pheasant hisses in a very snake-like manner if it becomes distressed or feels threatened.

During the late 18th century, the Chinese ringed-neck pheasant was introduced, with its neckband of 'pearls', and has interbred so successfully with the original species that today the sight of a pheasant without its pure white collar is rare. Necklaces of pearls are also associated with Mary Magdalene, because the pearl is the lunar jewel of wisdom and symbol of the origin of life (it has been proven that the Moon first nurtured life on Earth into being). Some people believe that, according to several evidential sources, there was a fourth wise man who brought pearls and sapphires from the Persian Gulf to honour the birth of Mary Magdalene, but that he was never allowed to reach the birth-place of the two Christ children. The mystical pheasant signifies feminine beauty and wisdom, feminine spirituality, joy, promise, nurturing, nourishment and mother love.

Greek legend tells us that Jason and his Argonauts brought the pheasant back with them from Georgia when they returned home after sailing in search of the Golden Fleece or the sacrificial ram knowledge ('ram' indicated the highest esoteric knowledge of the spirit, which is why it appears in many of the names of the Egyptian pharaohs, and why the great Hebrew patriarch and father of nations, Abram or Abraham [initially Avram] also bore it.) The fact that Jason came home with an approximation of the Feng bird is symbolic of his need to understand the origins of life and the deepest secrets of the spirit before he could 'put on' ram, or the Golden Fleece.

Sometimes, the presence of the augural pheasant warns against the masculine imbalances that occur in a limited understanding of ram (the 'lots of you equal only one of glorious me' philosophy concerning the pheasant's tendency to demand a harem, for instance) which need to be corrected before the bird's supremely favourable auspice can be realized. To dream of the pheasant is a sign of happy tidings, and a golden omen of harmonious plenty.

Phoenix (*see also* PHEASANT)

This beautiful bird of mythology (closely allied to the pheasant) succumbs to mortality only to declare its spiritual glory by bursting into flames and rising again from its own ashes once in every 500 years. The phoenix is also linked with the idea of the sacred serpent.

Mary Magdalene bears strong associations with the phoenix. The wondrous Star Temple at Glastonbury, where figures of the zodiac are delineated by natural features in a circular area around Glastonbury Tor, depicts a phoenix rising from its ashes as the sigil for the zodiacal tenancy of Aquarius. Prophets and seers say that this bird symbolizes Mary Magdalene, destined to rise from her enforced obscurity and come again in our own age. They say further that the chance to recognize her significance has been proffered to humanity every 500 years since the Crucifixion, and each time we have been too wilfully blind to accept the realization, but that this final chance will at last resonate with our developing collective soul.

Several old texts bear witness to the fact that Mary Magdalene landed in France about three years after the Crucifixion, with Mother Mary, Joseph of Arimathea and several of the original disciples, having been forced to flee from their homeland by Roman persecution. They came to Britain at the express invitation of the arch-Druid and his bishops, some months later, and built a little wattle-and-daub church where the Lady Chapel now stands within the ruins of Glastonbury Abbey. Mary Magdalene baptized tens of thousands in the pure inland waters of Glastonbury, which was called the Isle of Avalon in those days, and preached all over Britain before returning to France some years later. It was during this period that the pheasant – the Feng bird or the phoenix – began to walk the land. Mary Magdalene has long been known in esoteric circles as 'she who shall rise again'.

When all hope is gone and dreams are reduced to ashes, the wondrous phoenix glimmers on the brink of manifestation, ready to soar heavenwards to bring glorious resurgence to your life.

Pigeon (*see also* DOVE)

Although the pigeon bears strong associations and family ties with the dove, it has its own remarkable folklore. One legend, so well documented that it appears to have contained some truth, concerns Charles I, who suffered lawful death by decapitation and was succeeded by Oliver Cromwell. When Bernini's bust of the ill-fated monarch was brought home to be presented to Charles I, the king was sitting in the garden of Chelsea Palace. He ordered the sculpture to be uncovered and set up before him on the grass. At the very moment that the couriers did so, a hawk seized a pigeon overhead and a streak of blood fell on the neck of the bust. Although the servants hastened to remove it, the blood left an indelible stain.

The pigeon has served as a bird of sacrifice for millennia, and, as in this instance, will give of its own blood to issue warnings. Because of this divine aspect of the bird, and because the Holy Spirit took the form of a dove or a pigeon, in Russia it was considered a transgression to eat it or harm it in any way. It was the tradition for two pigeons to be released at a Russian wedding so that the newly married couple might be blessed by the Paraclete and inspired to be as faithful and self-sacrificing in their devotion as the pigeon.

Mohammad kept a pet pigeon, which he fed by placing corn in his ear so that the bird would put its beak inside it, as a symbol that he was inspired by the Holy Spirit; and consequently in Mecca no one will harm blue pigeons because they are considered sacred.

The black pigeons of Dodona took their flight from the city of Thebes in Egypt; one landed in Libya, the other in Dodona in ancient Greece. On the spot where the former alighted, the temple of Jupiter Ammon was erected. In the place where the other settled, the oracle of Jupiter was established; there the responses from the god to the supplicant were made via the black pigeons that inhabited the surrounding groves, and by brass plates suspended on the oak trees of Dodona, which, being struck by hanging thongs when the wind blew, gave forth a variety of mysterious and ghostly sounds like answering spirit-voices. The wellspring of the genesis of the renowned oracle in Dodona and the temple in Libya is that Jupiter presented his daughter Thebe with two mystical black pigeons which had the power of human speech. Lemprière states that the Greek word *peleiai* (pigeons) means 'old women' in the dialect of the Epirots (the people of the Epiros region where the Greek village of Dodona is located); so that the two black pigeons with human voices were representative of two black or African women. From these legends we can deduce that the pigeon is a sacred and oracular bird of both the supreme male and female deity, being associated with the Holy Spirit (Divine Mother) manifesting as the Black Virgin or Isis, and with Jupiter, greatest of the gods and Lord of Form in today's esoteric understanding.

Our feral pigeons today are descended from rock doves (they still love to roost and nest on the faces of buildings, just as their ancestors covered the rock faces), which are famous for their biblical appearance in the Song of Solomon, a spiritually erotic text telling of the mystic union of love between the feminine and masculine aspects of the Godhead, and focusing particularly on the black (hidden) aspect of Goddess: 'I am black, but I am beautiful,' she announces in the biblical poem. The rock-doves announce that the time is right for the union to commence. Pigeons roosting on the roof of a newly married couple foretell felicity, a long married life and many children. It is said that stolen pigeons will never mate, but if they are allowed to return to their original home they will mate again, even if several years have elapsed since their theft.

A swallow-tailed pigeon, particularly a white one, is a luck-bringer.

There is a wealth of unpleasant folklore concerning pigeon cures, most of which involve slicing a live bird in two, or treating it with even more severe cruelty, and placing it on the soles of the feet of one desperately injured or about to expire from illness. The concept behind this appalling treatment was one of sympathetic magic, whereby via the pigeon's sacrificial nature it would allow the disease or the right of the spirit of approaching death to demand the trophy of the life-spark to be transferred to itself, so saving the human victim.

Stories of the pigeon bearing a death omen prove that the bird generally delivers them in the benign spirit of a warning, which, if heeded, mercifully saves lives. A dove or a white pigeon flying round a pithead was a sure sign to miners of an impending disaster. In 1902, one was spotted fluttering around at a pit in Glyncarrwg in Glamorganshire, and 300 colliers immediately downed tools. No disaster occurred, but the miners were certain that, had they ignored the warning, lives would have been lost, simply because tales were legion of fatalities underground when white pigeons had been seen to make an appearance at a pit shortly beforehand.

We may think of pigeons as guardian spirits which seek to prevent disaster rather than bringers of death and sorrow. Charlotte Burne gives an intriguing account in her book, *Shropshire Folk-lore*, of two brown-and-white pigeons who came as guardian spirits to those who passed on whilst resident at Cayhowell Farm. Richard Gough, whose sister was the farmer's wife, reported that every time a member of the family fell into a decline, these birds arrived on the farm approximately a fortnight before death occurred, and flew away soon afterwards. He witnessed the event three times himself: once when Mrs Bradocke, the farmer's mother, died, then when his own father perished whilst staying at the farm, and finally when Andrew Bradocke, the farmer himself, expired from a fever. On each occasion the birds arrived without fail two weeks before the event, flew about the garden and yards, pecked at seeds and scraps, and generally behaved exactly like normal pigeons, except that at night they roosted under the shelter of the eaves, as if guarding the house through the watches of the night. They never appeared except during the fortnightly period before a death, and always left three days after it. The death of her husband affected Mrs Bradocke deeply, and when she herself fell ill some time afterwards, her apprehensive brother visited every day, dreading that the pigeons might appear once again. Thankfully, they did not, and Richard Gough was delighted to watch his sister recover her strength and become entirely well again. However, some years later, when she let the farm to a tenant, the poor man fell ill, the pigeons returned, and within two weeks he was dead.

Do not regard it as a death-omen if the pigeon makes itself known to you! The appearance of the bird is a fortunate sign, betokening its traditional happy influences – a happy and long-lived marriage or partnership, fertility, abundance, and felicity. The pigeon is an oracular bird, and bears messages from Mother God and Father God, from the supreme union of the Godhead. It is a bearer of the Holy Spirit, the Paraclete; and it signals the most judicious time for a love-affair, a partnership, a pregnancy, or some other project to be initiated, although it also indicates that a degree of self-sacrifice may be necessary in order to ensure its implementation and fruition.

Pink Flamingo

This beautiful, exotic bird gains its fairytale plumage from volcanic lakes and mineral spas which are warm and sulphurous. It has perfected what the storm petrel advocates (*see entry*) in that it has gleaned an angelic harvest from the hot, explosive points upon the Earth's surface. When we command the elemental furnaces within us in full consciousness of the directives of the spiritually-luminous soul, we shine with the beauty of the morning, with the poignancy of evening, and with the noon's full strength. No foul or dismal weather oppresses us, and no storms shake our foundations. The pink flamingo glows with the colour of the rose, which is an emblem of love both human and divine. This, and how it brings forth the yield of such supreme love, is the bird's enchanted augury.

Pintail (*see also* DUCK)

The pintail bears the same augury as the duck, with the added specification that the masculine and feminine aspects of emotion need to be dealt with separately, and their differences assimilated and understood, before harmonization and ultimate balance can be achieved.

Pipit

The pipit sings an augury of the sweetness of life throughout its highs and lows. It is the reassuring, affirmative voice of spring ever returning, of green shoots appearing once again in what might feel like a dead and withered landscape of the heart that you believed was trashed beyond all hope of resurrection.

If life seems galling, without appeal, let the little pipit help you to find the wellsprings of sweetness once again.

Meadow Pipit: this tiny bird of the meads counsels you to find replenishment out in nature; it bids you walk mindfully in wild places, consciously breathing the air and observing cloud formations and the handiwork of bush, flower and tree, so that you may restore yourself to yourself.

Rock Pipit: the rock pipit sings to ease your suffering, and reminds you that the stoniest trail leads to the highest peaks; it recognizes that the unrelenting facets of your nature, those which are hardest of all to change, constitute what presses so mercilessly on the tenderness of your soul, your inner being; it counsels you to bring about change by affirming and blessing the presence within you of those qualities you seem to lack, or are in negative opposite mode of those you sorely need. The rock pipit says: 'Ask, and it shall be given unto you.'

Tree Pipit: the tree pipit makes an appearance to show you that you will find healing and renewal by freeing, stimulating and feeding your imagination. Your imaginative qualities are about to become luminous, and to indicate the way forward out of the defile you have descended into.

Water Pipit: the delicate water pipit speaks to you of your emotions; there is no easy flow, and your feelings have become beleaguered and unexpressed, doing violence to your nerves and your sense of inner peace. Like a magician, let the little water pipit conjure the gentle flow of ethereal water through the blocks and resistances of your emotional suffering; think of soft, soothing movement, and an easy dispersal of knots of distress into a pure, effortless tide of healing that relaxes and replenishes as it entirely supports you and bears you up. Rest, trust and drift within the peace of this hushed, magical wash of water.

Plover (Grey) *(see also* GOLDEN PLOVER*)*

The grey plover comes to bring comfort when you have fallen in love 'by yourself'. Unreciprocated and unrequited love can become a crushing burden; the grey plover would inspire you to ease and gentle your grief by finding artistic expression of some sort as an outlet, no matter how inept you may consider your ability in this field. One of the saddest stories of art employed in this way concerns 'the Tear-Drop Room', still in existence on the second floor of 'The George' public house in Wallingford, England. Here a young woman, the landlord's daughter, who had seen her lover brutally murdered, had to be kept isolated in her room because the experience had unhinged her mind. To restore her sanity, she mixed her tears with soot from the chimney and painted row upon row of meticulously shaped and applied tear-drops upon the plaster walls. Although her tragedy occurred in 1626, part of one of the decorated walls is still in existence. Perhaps the spirit of the grey plover or the Kentish plover *(see below)*, seeing her grief, had drawn close to whisper the secrets of its wisdom to this tragic young woman and to bring her healing at last.

One strange and evocative folktale of the plover tells that it cries the name of the lost loved one as it wheels above the mourner wandering sorrowfully below.

Kentish Plover: Although the Kentish plover shares the same augury as the grey plover, it also emphasizes the need for solitude in order to heal. It comes to share the burden of that 'saddest of all lonelinesses', the loneliness experienced when a loved one is irrecoverably lost.

The Kentish plover cries: 'Through solitude, through going within, your lost loved one will be found again.'

Ringed Plover: The ringed plover comes to tell us that our grief has turned full circle, and that we must forsake solitude and turn away from the deadly temptation of self-perpetuating sorrow.

Pochard (*see also* DUCK)

The pochard is a small duck which spends most of its daylight hours sleeping, as it feeds at night. Its augury, in tandem with that of the duck in general, points to the need to allow deep-seated emotional disturbances to emerge and express themselves through dream symbolism. The pochard comes to alert us to these hidden emotional issues, and to signal that they are ready to surface in our dream life. Wise masters will come to us in our dreams to help us to resolve our painful schisms and imbalances and will offer guidance, via our dreaming consciousness, which will help us to steer from the boiling rapids toward clear, still waters of the soul. Keep a dream journal in the period directly following the pochard's appearance, and allow your imagination to take full flight as far as understanding and interpreting your dreams is concerned.

Pochard (Red-Crested) (*see also* DUCK and POCHARD)

The larger, red-crested pochard usually sports a glow of orange on top of its head, as though a soft light, within the skull, lit up its sombre brown head-feathers at this point.

The augury of the red-crested pochard is interesting, because it announces that the time is ripe for rich harvesting as far as dream imagery, interpretation and revelation is concerned. What is given forth from your dreams at this point will not only bring healing and reconciliation, but contains the potential to transform and invigorate the entire panorama of your life. Receiving the red-crested pochard into your vision as a wisdom bird is a powerful and a royally-favoured portent. Keep a dream journal beside your bed and record your dreams assiduously.

During this journey of beautifully auspiced discovery, the red-crested pochard may appear to you briefly as black-capped. This is its 'eclipse' plumage, which the male moults into after breeding. It is flightless during this period, but after a few weeks it regains its bright feathers and is airborne again. The black-capped, 'eclipsed' pochard signals that for a short time the enchanted lanterns shining into the fabulous caverns of dream will go out. Your dream life will remain just as important, but you will remember nothing of it. During this 'eclipsed' period, eat lightly, and consume only pure, natural foods. Allow yourself eight hours in bed each night, so that your blacked-out dreams may continue to write their hidden script as you sleep. It is from this 'dark of the moon' that the greatest dream revelation will eventually emerge.

Ptarmigan

The ptarmigan is a beautiful, dove-like bird of the high mountain peaks. It turns pure white in winter, with the exception of the under-feathers of the tail. This signifies that although it seeks the mountain-tops of spiritual vision and understanding, it remains firmly rooted into the good earth, which gives the high-flyer humility, grounded perception and a broad-seated benevolence.

The ptarmigan holds up for us the symbol of the black spot of sacred darkness as the root and the source of the outflowing light. It counsels all high-flyers, in whatever arena of endeavour, to remember this wisdom.

Puffin

The delightful 'clown' of the bird colonies that breed amongst the rocks, this unusual bird with its strangely flattened, colourful bill and its stately walk, comes to us to emphasize the importance of humour and self-knowing. Its strange growling call sounds like burlesque laughter, and its spiritual presence lampoons our deepest held convictions of self-importance.

Its name derives from its 'puffed-up' appearance, a comical mirroring of the conceit that it loves to deflate in those to whom it comes as augur. Despite its love of parody and judicious levelling, the spirit of the puffin is kindly and nurturing. If it knocks us down, it helps us back up, newly unburdened of our blinding conceits. As its vivid, big-top-esque eye-patches reveal, it loves to spotlight our blinkers and then, with its hoarse, pisky laughter, disabuse us of them!

Its peculiar, mirthful call rasps: 'Get real!'

Quail

Britain's only migratory game bird, the diminutive quail with its strange cry is mystically associated with the Sun and with the oak tree, even though it is a bird of the grassy plains. Sacred to Apollo, it was also a symbol of Melkarth, the Phoenician Sun god, who, like Persephone, was also a god of the underworld until summer's return. The red-haired Phoenicians were associated in ancestry with the early Britons and the Celts, and it is interesting that the oak, the supreme druidic emblem, was sign and symbol of Melkarth. British people were once known as 'men-of-oak'. Arthur, the great 6th-century king who was counselled by the arch-Druid Merlin, was said by the monks of Glastonbury Abbey, when they disinterred his body, to be a giant of a man whose coffin was a natural, hollowed-out oaken tree-trunk; and Merlin, Prince of Enchanters, is believed to dwell at the heart of a hollow oak tree in the Caledonian forest, sealed in by Nimue, the enchantress, and awaiting the day when he will re-emerge to guide and enlighten the sovereign of Britain once more.

When the quail is seen again in late March, the oak is said to begin to unfurl its buds to welcome its return and to celebrate the principle of resurrection in honour of the Sun deity. Resurrection is indeed the meaning and message of the secretive quail, which hides away and calls enchantingly from the long grass.

Because it was a bird symbolic of the sacred sex ceremony, enacted between ancient kings and queens of forgotten cultures, wherein the king was afterwards ritually 'slain' (thankfully, this part of the ceremony was sometimes relegated to the realm of theatre only, and the king actually survived the ritual), to be resurrected the following morning at sunrise, the innocuous little quail has been branded as a bird reminiscent of lasciviousness and prostitution! Yet resurrection is the promise it brings; a renewal of the heart's mysteries and energies so that that ultimate centre strengthens its root in its origin – the Divine – and grows sturdy and steadfast as the heart of the oak.

Whilst the oak and the Sun deity were generally regarded as masculine, the quail is a rain bird, a bird of Goddess. Its eggs were served as a ritual meal prior to the sacred sex ceremony, for they were, in their magical essence, eggs of wisdom, of divinely renewed life, of resurrection itself. They contained the little serpent that would become the golden erect life-force known in the East as 'kundalini', although the concept of the kundalini does not entirely embrace the full mystery of the resurrection.

In later centuries quail eggs, due to their history, became a great delicacy, eaten only by the 'élite', although the exclusiveness surrounding them was a vulgarization of their true significance, for their connection with nobility was of the heart, and not one of rank.

Like the pheasant, the quail is a sacrificial bird and is linked with the phoenix. It will give of itself when the need arises, as is stated in the biblical Exodus, where on two occasions migratory flocks of quails in evening flight covered the camp of the starving Israelites, alighting everywhere and ready for the taking. This quality of sudden ubiquity is evident today in the quail's ventriloquist skills. It can throw its voice to trick sportsmen, although this unusual gift is also said to denote its enchantress qualities. When the female sounds her call, the male 'worships' her by dancing the sacred ring around her, elongating his throat and puffing up his neck and breast feathers as he drags his wings along the ground in courtship. In the mythology of the quail, this behaviour is believed to be an enactment of the king offering himself in sacrifice, as his ritual death would involve the tying of his hands behind his back and the death-blows would fall upon his neck and breast.

It was also believed that long ago in the Golden Age, when Earth was a paradise, quail once lived beside running waters, although it is now confined to dry grasslands. As a firebird, sacred to the Sun, it awaits the day when the old ceremonies will be seen and understood in the light of their true significance, and the sacred waters of life will spring again in human consciousness, relieving its parched thirst. Until this happy time comes, it cries unseen from the long grass: 'Wet-my-lips, wet-my-lips, wet-my-lips', hidden, as John Clare remarks in his poem 'Summer Moods' (and with remarkable insight regarding the quail's history, philosophy and prophecy), 'as thoughts unborn'.

Its augury is one of resurrection, of the blessings of Goddess, of the sacredness of sex, of the strident qualities of the masculine principle deferring to the heart-wisdom of the feminine principle, of a renewal of strength and purpose, of generously supplying where there is need, and of triumphantly outwitting and rebutting predatory intent without retaliation or ill will.

Rail (Water) *(see also* CRAKE (SPOTTED))

This attractive little marsh bird, smaller than the moorhen, which trails its legs in flight like a diminutive heron, can be distinguished from its cousin the spotted crake by its long slender red beak. The water rail comes to us to literally 'rail' at us regarding a message from our higher selves that we have been stubbornly disregarding!

The water rail is shy and secretive, remaining invisible within the reeds and knot-grass of the lonely marshes whilst ever it fears a negative or a predatory reception, and yet is ready to remain prominently in sight and even becomes quite confident and friendly once it is sure its appearance will not be abused. In like manner, the augural spirit of this little water bird will remain uniformly insistent as soon as we admit its message and its manifestation into our consciousness. It will not give up until we begin to act on its advice!

To discern its message with clarity, we must once again seek to gaze into those 'inner pools of reflection and contemplation, which become still and clear when we allow ourselves a period of quiet time and mindfulness to study their depths'. Within the mystery of this inner water, the augural message of the persistent little water rail will take vivid form. In contemplating this revelation, however, we must not forget the bird's long, probing beak. Once it has delivered its message, it asks you to probe deeper, to thoroughly explore and generally have a good poke around in those inner pools of vision and awareness! You are sure to come up with interesting and unexpected finds which will cast unconventional and surprising illumination on your current situation, your abilities, your potentialities, your opportunities, your life-path.

The water rail has an astonishing cry. Not only does it emit a variety of grunts and squeals, but its clearest call is an elongated piercing squeal like that of a piglet! 'Expect the unexpected' is the water rail's motto, 'for nothing is beyond the bounds of possibility!' Look out for flying pigs!

Raven

Odin, the great Norse god, bore the sacred ravens Hugin and Munin (Mind and Memory) on his shoulders. These birds of wisdom would fly out over the world each day, and return to their master to tell him of all they saw. 'The Fatal Raven', consecrated to Odin, was the emblem on the Danish standard. This raven was believed to be in possession of necromantic power. The standard was known as *Landeyda* ('the desolation of the country'), and miraculous powers were attributed to it.

The Fatal Raven was the device of Odin, god of triumphs, and was said to have been woven and embroidered in a single noontide under deep enchantment by the daughters of Regnor Lodbrok, son of Sigurd, a mighty warrior who chanted his intrepid death song – the *Krakamal* – whilst being bitten to death in a loathsome pit filled with deadly vipers. If the Danish arms were destined to suffer defeat, it was said that the raven emblazoned on the standard drooped his wings. If, on the other hand, victory was to be their portion, he stood erect and soaring, as if inviting the warriors to follow.

Later superstition attributed unpleasant omens and symbols to the raven, among them pestilence, cruelty, foulness, greed, death, the devil, misfortune, bitter and prolonged war, wickedness and plunder; the collective noun 'sadness' is given to ravens. These doleful associations are made largely because the raven is a bird of carrion and is entirely jet-black.

A more balanced view might see the raven as a servant of the life-forces. It strips away unwanted and time-worn conditions, clearing and cleansing the field of life for new dispensations to take root. This may seem like cruelty, rapaciousness and foulness, but is actually quite the opposite; and so we find that in the older mythologies, which were gifted with a clearer vision of the eternal verities, the raven is a bird of divine knowledge and wisdom, sacred to Asclepius, the Greek god of healing, and to Apollo the Sun god, the great patron of augurs, who was one of the primordial teachers of the Language of the Birds, instructing humanity how to 'foretell' through observation and attunement to birds, not only future events, but the life and dimensions of the soul.

Before he availed himself personally of the wisdom of ravens, Apollo had denounced the entire raven race and condemned it to darkness, because a raven had prophesied that a certain nymph, with whom he was in love, would deceive the great Sun god and make a fool of him. The prophecy was correct, but simply because the poor bird had brought him bad tidings, Apollo decided to cast it and its kind into everlasting night, barring it from the palace of the Sun and from wearing its former paradise-white plumage. His wrath also extended to diminishing its size. Prior to his curse, ravens had been as big as eagles, but were deprived of their royal status and stature when they were doomed to wear black, their mourning-clothes as birds of sorrow.

Long before the coming of Apollo the raven had been a symbol of the prophesying foreknowledge that so enraged the sun god, and was the companion of Bran the Blessed, god of the underworld and secret knowledge, who is a guardian of Britain. ('Bran' means 'raven'.) His 'head' or consciousness is said to be buried on Tower Hill, protecting the country. Bran's ravens inhabit the Tower of London (the tower is a powerful feminine symbol), and if they should ever vacate it, it is said that dire calamity will fall upon Britain. Here the raven is in the guise of protector, not bringing death and destruction but shielding from it. Perhaps this is why the raven's egg (its essence) is said to contain the soul of King Arthur, who will, one day when the time is right, come forth reborn to save the soul of the world from overwhelming darkness.

This may be the root of the real truth about the raven. The 'Raven-Woman' was often seen in the dreams of the Celtic shaman, bringing wisdom, healing and enlightenment.

A wider understanding of 'The Fatal Raven' might decipher its connection to the three feminine Fates, the mystic sisters who spin, weave, and finally cut the threads of each individual human life, not as an act of destruction but as a gift of liberation into the bright worlds of the spirit after a period of labour within this earthly school for souls.

I have always felt that the raven is a benign bird secreting great beauty in the blackness of its aspect, like a dark angel whose presence causes dread until it throws off its cloak of night to reveal the marvellous jewel of brilliant lustral light that is its essence. This essence remains hidden from the blindness of mundane and superficial vision which, in its own lightlessness, judges the majestic spirit of the raven as dark and dreadful. Its secret is that it knows that death, war, pestilence and suffering are the four great cornerstones of the temple of human consciousness in wrong manifestation, for in reality they are their opposites – undiminishing life, brotherhood, well-being and limitless healing. It is we ourselves who distort, pervert, corrupt and blaspheme these beautiful and divine energies into the Four Horsemen of Doom. Until humanity will agree to emerge from its own blinkered darkness and put on its true inheritance, the raven must keep house in the temple as we are choosing to express it, and the resonances it is consequently condemned to watch over cast it into the mode of a bird of sorrow, although it counteracts even this inescapable role with its love of humour!

The true calibre of the raven is acknowledged in the recognition that it is a sustainer of life, carrying nourishment to Elijah in the desert when he fled the rage of Ahab, and also bringing sustenance to the saints Anthony, Apollonaris, Benedict, Oswald, Paul the Hermit, and Vincent.

Historical reports of the raven attest to many marvels. Jovianus Potanus tells of two skirmishes between ravens and kites near Beneventum, noted by many people, which proved to be the prognostication of a great battle. Nicetas speaks of a similar fracas between crows and ravens as 'presaging the irruption of the Scythians into Thrace'. He also reported that his friend Draper, 'in the flower of his age and robust health, knew he was at the point of death because two ravens flew into his chamber'. Cicero was forewarned of his demise by the persistent fluttering of ravens, and Macauley relates a legend that a raven entered the chamber of the renowned orator on the morning of the day of his murder and pulled back the bedclothes!

Again, we note that the raven brings warnings, sacrificing its own safety and well-being in an effort to either persuade us to take heed and escape danger, to forearm us by forewarning, or to escort our soul to the spheres beyond as a guardian spirit if our destiny decrees our death.

Recent extensive research has proven that ravens are highly intelligent, have a keen sense of humour, and demonstrate deep and faithful bonds of attachment with human beings as well as their own kind. Their great powwows as they sit upon the ground in council, their numbers sometimes extending across several arable fields or acres of moorland, are an impressive and unearthly sight, as is their evening homeward flight, when they are said to call the global news of the day to one another as they sail to their roosts.

Noah availed himself of the wisdom of the raven when he sought dry land from the Ark, and the great god of time, called both Saturn and Cronos, has a raven as companion and symbol.

We may think of the raven as bringing us the night to show us the stars, or, more mundanely, as those moments of blackness we sit through when watching a film. A substantial portion of any one hour of cinematic film contains these dark moments, although we don't notice them whilst watching the images. Without them, the film would be an incoherent focus of blinding light, impossible to watch. This perfect blending of the darkness and the light in the raven can bring us a deep healing called 'the resolution of opposites', wherein profound conflicts, long held within us, are brought into harmony. This is why the raven is associated with the Sun gods Apollo and Lugh, and was anciently regarded as the morning bird of joy and light. His croak says: 'Bless your shadow-self with the light of Love!'

When the raven comes to you, he brings the 'raven-knowledge' of the solar brotherhood of the Druids, and bids you give ear to the 'Raven-Woman' within you who will dispense wisdom and healing, preparing you for your next important initiation in the sacred cycle of your life.

Razorbill

The black-and-white razorbill, with its beak blunt and rounded as if carefully tooled, bids us take into philosophical consideration the broad stretches of the levels of life, and the vast profundity of its deeps. It would encourage us to harmonize and balance the two, not to make shades of grey out of the seeming black-and-white polarities of existence, but to express what truly lies between the absolute absorption of light and the absolute radiation of light (black and white), which of course is the whole glorious colour spectrum!

The razorbill advises us not to bury ourselves in the profundities of life to the extent that we become anxious and depressed about major issues, for we will better find the answer to them when we emerge to dance upon the levels and express light-heartedness in the living of our lives.

It counsels us just as earnestly not to lose ourselves in a wilderness of trivia and mundane or sensational superficiality, for by so doing we starve our soul, abuse our spirit and lose sight of the grand purpose of our lives. Striking the right balance between life's depths and surfaces will smooth our sharp corners!

The blunt-billed razorbill dives deep, and has been recorded at depths of 140 metres below sea level. It spends most of its life far out at sea, bobbing on the surface of the water when it is not flying or diving. Its call is a guttural 'car-rrr', the old English word for a large, low-lying, level stretch of land reclaimed from water.

It cries: 'Dive for pearls, and do not be afraid to strike deep to find them; but remember that you cannot enjoy their gifts of beauty and wonder on the ocean bed, but in the world of everyday above!'

Redpoll (Common and Lesser) (see FINCH)

Redshank

The shrewd redshank would have us contemplate the red and the white squares of the traditional chessboard. If we seek inspiration for the spiritual meaning of the game of kings from Lewis Carroll and his famous *Through the Looking-Glass and What Alice Found There*, we find that the Red Queen is rather formidable, whilst the White Queen is rather foolish! In the end, of course, Alice herself becomes queen, and manages to balance both aspects of the red (the will) and white (the heart) worlds she has encountered.

In another sense, the redshank asks us to look at the sympathetic and parasympathetic aspects of the nervous system. Our sympathetic nervous system is our 'fight or flight' mechanism. It is fuelled by protein and charges up our 'nerves' to a high pitch. The parasympathetic mode takes effect when we are tranquil, ready to settle down and relax. If there is imbalance between the two, we will either be full of fear, stress and wrath, like the Red Queen, or, like the White Queen we may feel indolent and lean towards indulgence.

The heart becomes the true centre of inner guidance when the will does not disconnect from it, but bends its knee in honour of the principle of love and is absorbed into the heart as a purified energy, becoming attuned to the higher self. It is at this point that the two modes of the nervous system work together in perfect harmony to achieve the peaceful, heart-centred individual.

If you are either nervy or listless, the redshank urges you to seek the point of balance in the heart, which can be achieved by learning to meditate and by control of the breath via the art of gentle, regulated breathing-cycles undertaken for a few moments several times each day. By attuning peacefully to the heart in this way, we become queen or king of our own lives, and are no longer pulled helplessly in opposite directions by the undisciplined reactions of our will and our emotions.

The fiery red indicator of the will is expressed in the redshank by its name, the vivid orange base of its bill, by its orange-red legs and by its general nerviness, which it expresses loudly in true 'fight or flight' manner by being the first to alert other birds in the vicinity to danger with its high-pitched cry. That its true message advocates the supreme monarchy of the heart, however, is shown clearly by the white V (the sign of the heart) extending along its back, and by its display posture, which it assumes after gliding to the ground, whereon it stands still with pinions raised to exhibit its white under-wing feathers. Its cry exhorts: 'Find the point of peace within, and avert a crisis!'

Redshank (Spotted) *(see also* REDSHANK)

The augural message is similar to that of the redshank – quiet attunement to the balancing wisdom of the heart which addresses stresses within the personality – with the addition that the spotted redshank brings an augury of baptism. This might mean that your belief system will change or that you undergo some purificatory ritual, either spiritual in tone or brought about by life-events. A rebirth may take place within you. You will be submerged in an element which cleanses, gives new life and allows you to cast off your old self. This could be a religion, a philosophy, a spiritual awakening, a journey into your creative self, a birth, a life-changing opportunity, or a relationship.

Redstart

The redstart's face is obscured by a black shadow (an attractive feature of this bright little bird, which is about the size of a robin), but its heart and tail, the latter indicative of the power of the mind, are fiery and radiant.

Some hidden influence is about to make itself felt, or someone is about to come into your life whom you will be unable to penetrate or read clearly, but whose heart and mind are good, and who will bring you a truly enriching happiness.

The redstart's tail bobs up and down continually, and its energies are ever at high-water mark, denoting the quicksilver current of the mind and its power of freeing, revitalizing and transforming blocked and stifled inner forces. The redstart's augury has the power to bring lasting joy if its recipient will consent to be guided by the spirit of this bird.

Occasionally it foretells a breakthrough in your own life whereby your gifts of mind and heart are at last recognized and paid due tribute. Its rich, jubilant warble sings: 'Judge by the fruits, not by the roots!'

127

Redstart (Black) (see REDSTART)

In the case of the black redstart the issue is cloudier than that augured by the redstart. Obscuration certainly exists, but the radiance of the redstart belongs here only to the tail (indicative of the mind). These alluring mental energies can be tricky, as they can attract, where, if their true nature were known, they would repel. The mind, full of its own intellectual and analytical importance, can be a fool. It can think that it is being enriched by the pure power of imagination, whereas it is being led on a merry dance of deception and fantasy. It has to return with humility to the heart, and bend its knee to her wisdom, before it can be set on course once more.

The black redstart symbolizes one of those rare instances where shades of grey exist between the two polarities of black and white, rather than the full colour spectrum. You will receive nothing but wise counsel if you remind yourself that the glass is half empty as well as half full. All may look brightly shining, all lights may seem to be green, but the black redstart advises caution. Check things out, not only by removing rose-tinted spectacles, but by positively assuming a pair that are slightly grey-tinted! They will bring things back into perspective.

The call of this urgent little bird is literally an exclaiming 'tucc, tucc!', rather like a loud and insistent tutting!

Redwing

Smaller and more delicate than the song thrush, but similar in its habits, the shy and retiring redwing flies into your field of vision to encourage you to put on display your talents and gifts, of the mind, of the spirit, of the hands, of vision both soaring and solidly practical. Whatever arena they involve, it is time to be an exhibitionist, in the best sense!

The delightful redwing is a mime artist. It has a boldly-striped face, yet chooses to be rarely seen. Its flanks and underwings show a flash of red, yet it is a secretive bird which is exceedingly careful not to draw attention to itself. It carries a thrush inheritance, but its song is seldom heard. When it does sing, although it is not a nocturnal bird, it often sings after dark.

REDSTART (BLACK) – ROBIN

In creating this theatre of opposites, it teaches us that to be in possession of all these attributes, and yet to act contrary to their nature and their purpose, is to allow the grapes to wither on the vine. The redwing would remind us of the parable of the talents, whereby the cautious, secretive, guarded man who buried his talents for safekeeping was proven to be on a road to nowhere. Prudence and caution should be our servants, not our jailors! The redwing's cry is: 'Be bold! Move forward! Go for it! Rise on fiery wings to the heights!'

Robin

This little bird, so friendly to humans, is the Bringer of the Sacred Fire. It is conspicuous at Christmas, when the Sun seems to turn in his course, and the life-giving light returns. The robin is also the bird of the New Year, a bright flame for our fortunes to confidently follow.

Rumour suggests that the early scarlet coats of postmen, and the colour of the pillar boxes that followed some time later, were inspired by the robin, the bearer of good tidings.

The poet Tekahionwake, a Mohawk princess born of an English mother and a Native Canadian Mohawk chief of the royal bloodline of Hiawatha, writing at the end of the 19th century, penned a soliloquy to the robin:

> Music, music with throb and swing,
> Of a plaintive note, and long;
> 'Tis a note no human throat could sing,
> No harp with its dulcet golden string –
> Nor lute, nor lyre with liquid ring,
> Is sweet as the robin's song.
>
> He sings for love of the season
> When the days grow warm and long,
> For the beautiful God-sent reason
> That his breast was born for song.

129

Calling, calling so fresh and clear,

Through the song-sweet days of May;

Warbling there, and whistling here,

He swells his voice on the drinking ear,

On the great, wide, pulsing atmosphere

Till his music drowns the day.

He sings for love of the season

When the days grow warm and long,

For the beautiful God-sent reason

That his breast was born for song.

A beautiful Native American legend called The Origin of the Robin tells how, in the long, long ago of the world, an elderly man had an only son, Iadilla. (The name is noteworthy because of its closeness to Homer's Iliad ['journey'], and indeed it describes the remarkable spiritual voyage undertaken by a foolish father and a tutelary son.)

When Iadilla came of age and was ready to make the lengthy and final fast that secured throughout life the company of a guardian genius or spirit, his father told him a secret. He explained that he believed Iadilla had it in him to greatly surpass all others in his attainment of the power and the knowledge and the sacred mysteries of the tribe. To achieve his potential, it would be necessary for him to fast for much longer than even those who held highest office had accomplished during their own coming-of-age ceremony.

To prepare for this great ritual, the father directed his son to go repeatedly to the sweating-lodge and bath so that the lustral rites he performed therein might make him ready for communion with his good spirit. He should then recline on a clean mat waiting in a little lodge which had been specially prepared for him. He was encouraged to summon all his strength to endure the fast, and assured that when twelve days had passed, food would be brought to him and he would receive the blessing of his father.

Iadilla obeyed, and spent his days stretched out on the sleeping-mat with his face covered, serenely awaiting the approach of his good spirit. Every morning his father came to the door of the little lodge and whispered encouragement to him, urging him to persevere and reminding him of the unconscionable honour and fame he would win in life if he was successful in enduring to the end.

Iadilla listened calmly, keeping silent until the ninth day, when he told his father that his dreams of the previous night bore an evil portent and that he sought permission to break his fast, and resume it at a better-auspiced time. His father urged him to complete his mission, reminding him that he had only three days more to endure, and that all glory would then be his. Iadilla was persuaded, and continued on until the eleventh day. His evil dreams still haunted him, however, and he again put his request to break his fast to his father, who repeated his remonstrances, and promised his son that he himself would prepare a fine meal and bring it to him at dawn the following morning. When Iadilla expressed distress at his father's unrelenting stance, the old man reproached him with wanting to bring shame upon him in his last years. On hearing these words, Iadilla promised to remain where he was until the next morning.

When his father came to the lodge at first light, having prepared a generous repast to revive his son, he was astonished to hear Iadilla talking earnestly to himself behind the door. He peered through a small aperture to see Iadilla lit with a strange spirit-light as if covering his chest with bright vermilion paint. Iadilla spoke as though he repeated the words of an invisible presence who was conversing with him. His words told how his father had destroyed his son's fate and fortune as a man because he had refused to listen to Iadilla's prophetic words concerning the evil tidings of his dreams, which meant that he had turned a deaf ear to the wisdom of the spirits. The spirits had seen that Iadilla was being forced beyond his tender strength, and had urged the heroic young man to be merciful to himself, break his fast, and attempt the ordeal again once his fortitude had matured a little.

'Now I shall be eternally happy in my new state,' continued Iadilla, 'for I have been an obedient son. My father alone will suffer, because my guardian spirit is a just one. Though he cannot now be propitious to me in the way I had desired, he has blessed me in a different way. He has given me another shape; and now I must go.'

The old man then broke into the room, crying, 'My son! My son! Do not leave me!' He thought he saw Iadilla lying dead upon the sleeping-mat; but in a scintilla of time his son had flown to the roof of the lodge and alighted on its topmost pole, having been transformed into a beautiful robin red-breast. Knowing that the old man had never intended him any harm, but had been led astray by the allure of pride and ambition, he looked down upon his father with the light of compassion in his eyes, and said, 'Regret not, dear father, the transformation you behold. I shall drink deeper of joy in my present state than could ever have been my lot as a man. I shall ever be the good friend of humankind and will always keep close to their dwellings. I will be eternally happy and serene; and although my fate has decreed that I could not be a famous and mighty warrior as you wished, it will daily be my aim to make you amends for it as a harbinger of peace and joy. I will bring you good cheer with my songs and strive to inspire in the breasts of all who hear me the jubilance and lightsomeness of heart I feel in my present state. May this prove some consolation to you for the loss of all the glory you anticipated. I am now free forever from the cares and burdens of human life. My food is spontaneously furnished by the mountains and the fields, and my path of life is in the bright air.'

Then stretching himself on his toes as if delighting in his gift of wings, Iadilla carolled one of his sweetest songs and took flight into a neighbouring wood, leaving his stricken father to weep after his loss, and, through his grief, to realize that his son had indeed greatly surpassed all others in his attainment of the power and the knowledge and the sacred mysteries of the tribe. From then on the mystical robin red-breast became a revered totem bird for Iadilla's people, offering spirit guidance and revelation through their medicine men and women.

The motifs in this story are interesting, because they involve the themes of mercy, compassion, obedience to the highest principles, resurrection and self-sacrifice, as do all legends of the robin world-wide. The robin is thus strongly associated with charity, and one legend attributes its flaming breast to singeing from the fires of purgatory as it mercifully brought water to ease the thirst of the suffering souls therein.

We should not forget, in this context, the redoubtable Robin Hood, whose mythological counterpart was Robin Goodfellow. ('Robin' is a derivative of Robert and means 'bright renown'.) Robin Hood, a sworn Templar Knight, returned from the lamentable Crusades with a deep sense that nowhere in the world were the true values of the ageless wisdom that Christ had taught abided by. To right this situation, he lived close to the sacred oak in the purity of the greenwood (there exists a complex of warm, dry caves beneath Nottingham Forest, which he made his home), and dedicated his life to self-sacrifice, love of his fellows, the protection of the poor and needy, and reverence for the sacred feminine. As stories of him tell, merriment and good cheer abounded in his camp – the mark of the true robin!

Another fable of the robin tells of how it tried to pull the thorns from the head of Christ as he hung on the Cross, and was stained by his blood; yet another claims that when the robin flew to fetch fire for humanity from the raging fires of the underworld, its breast took fire in the process. In Guernsey, the people used to say that there was no fire on the island until the robin brought it to them.

It is also an escorter of souls to paradise or the Summerlands, and is said to tenderly bury the bodies of any human being for whom this office has not been performed, so laying them to rest.

The joyful notes of the robin's song signify confiding trust, triumph, and happiness in love, and when it comes to you, as well as these things, it brings a merciful burying and laying-to-rest of old problems, old conflicts, old issues and old selves which need to be declared dead and buried so that your life-path is clear for forward movement; the red-breasted robin offers itself as guide, bearing before you a light from the angels to quicken the speed of your journeying soul.

Rook

The rook is a bird of benign omen, bringing benevolent fortune to humankind. Its cry has a strange beauty, sounding the voice of wild heights, high winds and the mysterious spirit of the land. The rook brings intimations to you of your own wildness: not uncontrolled self-gratification, which erects a prison around the soul, but the true, sweet wildness of our human spirit, which was given to us as part of our essence and which cannot be denied and forgotten without divesting us of our dignity, beauty and freedom – our spiritual wings.

The rook is also a spirit guardian and escorter of souls to the higher worlds. A case was reported in 2008 where a friendly rook popped through the cat flap and remained a visitor in the house until one of its occupants passed over, benignly ignored by the family cat! After the death had occurred, the rook also took flight.

However, although it befriends and serves human souls ready to pass over in this way, there is no need to regard the rook as an omen of death. I had a tame rook which came into my life in an unusual way, and I can certainly confirm that no deaths took place in the vicinity, either before, during or after it had passed out of my care. One day I will tell the full story of this remarkable and tutelary bird, which drew back many curtains for me on the Bright Knowledge, the radiance hidden within and behind the sacred darkness.

The rook's rousing call says: 'Rise on wings of the spirit to our high places in the thrilling wilderness of the wind! Leave behind your mind-routines and all mundane and mechanical perception, and come and dwell with us awhile!'

Rosefinch (Scarlet) *(see also* FINCH)

Whilst the scarlet rosefinch is included under the finch heading, it also has its own separate augury, given when it appears individually rather than communally with its other finch brethren. Its message is sweet and radiant. It brings a promise of love, and its symbol is the rose.

This enchanting little bird brings new meaning to Burns' immortal lines 'My love is like a red, red, rose / That's newly sprung in June.' The poet was referring to a woman, which bears its own truth regarding the practical meaning and the profoundest reaches of the significance of the rose. Yet the scarlet rosefinch comes to us to teach us how to make our love – the love we give forth – eternally as the 'red, red rose that's newly sprung in June'. Meditate deeply on this symbol of the rose, and you will understand the everlasting message of the rosefinch.

Its call is a persistent 'chew-ee, chew-ee, chew-ee', a phonetic representation in song of the heart of the word 'intuition' ('tuition from within'), which is a name for the sacred wisdom of the heart.

Ruff

This remarkable, exotic bird cuts a fine figure in the summer, when the male of the species sports a particularly dashing ruff which can be black and speckled (somewhat like that of a turkey), an impressive snow-white, or even a flashy orange. The female is a much more sober and sensible creature, resembling a redshank in its winter plumage.

The handsome ruff in all its finery (even if rather unimaginatively named!) brings an augur of earthly royalty, earthly nobility, culture and the upper echelons of society. You may find yourself rubbing shoulders with wealthy and famous people. However, there is likely to be a great deal of cut and thrust, a certain jostling for position. The energies, attitudes and values abroad in such society may alarm you as well as enthrall you and command your respect.

The ruff advises that you remain grounded in a strong sense of your own principles and your own worth. It also warns you to differentiate between what is truly admirable, and what is gross and commonplace wrapped in an outer layer of resplendent pomp and circumstance. Oddly enough, the ruff is also a symbol of the archetypal poet. It counsels you to enjoy what is on offer, but to remain attuned to your higher mind and to a genuine appreciation of real beauty.

Sanderling

Small, well-rounded and enthusiastic, there is something about this irrepressible little wader that suggests it almost might have been wound up, like a clockwork toy, and set upon the beach to dash around with a mechanical vigour and an inexorable energy as it searches for food along the shoreline.

Like the redwing, it comes to us to mimic the drama of our own inner dynamics. As restless as the waves, it courts and marshals the elemental forces of the sea like a tiny Triton. It will appear in your soul's vision when a dramatic release of energy is about to be triggered within you in response to some new and creative situation that will soon declare itself. It is important to remember that a crisis can be transformed into a potent opportunity, although a crisis is by no means necessarily in store for you. Whatever it is, you have the resources and the wherewithal to rise to the challenge, and it will give you joy to do so.

Sometimes the sanderling comes to us when we are embroiled in the middle of a demanding situation and experiencing a subsequent energy-release. In either case, it reminds us with its mimicry that when we drive ourselves too hard, our expression of energy tends to become mechanical and our responses mundane. We snap into a machine-like mindset. This is dehumanizing and unhealthy. The busy sanderling would remind us that we need to take a little time once or twice each day to halt our frantic output and gently enter into meditation. If we refuse to do this, our energy-field becomes gross and toxic, a potentially destructive force.

The sanderling counsels us to think of the sea. The endless waves manifest restlessness, rootlessness, inappeasability, until we attune to their breath-like rhythm and thereby step properly into their life-flow. Thereafter, all that is frenetic is absorbed into peace, and we are connected to our source.

The sanderling cries: 'Cattle are driven! Claim your birthright, and refuse to allow yourself to be driven!'

Sandpiper (All Types)

Ancient Native American lore tells of the sand spirits, who dwelt in the heart of the Earth and who disappeared even from this sacred abyss to enter into the Dream Worlds for six months of each year. In the Native American story, the benign sand spirits seek a mortal to marry one of their kind so that he can restore to them the holy tobacco, blessed by the Great Spirit, which will enable them to enter into the dominion of dreams during the six months that they remain in their earthly home.

> Wandering on the sands to cook a supper of fish, and anxious not to wake his cousin nearby who has fallen into a special state of divine sleep which has escorted him into the deepest magic of the Dream Worlds so that a door opens between dimensions, a young brave attaches a flaming torch to his forehead to enable him to perform the task of cooking supper alone. Seeing this fire-plume and recognizing the spiritual symbol that it constitutes (the radiance of the brow and crown centres, which indicate enlightenment), three beautiful sand-spirit maidens draw close and take him back with them to their secret lodge in the beauty of the underworld.

There he marries the youngest, and procures the divine tobacco from his own world of which the sand spirits stand so much in need. In doing this, he is challenged by an evil spirit who wishes to destroy the sand spirits, and, with them, humanity's vital connection to the Dream Worlds and all the life-essence, enchantment, and soul-nurturing and magical mandalas of colour-rays that they provide.

Staying close by his wife's side (not departing from the source of heart-wisdom) whilst the evil spirit attempts to wreak his worst vengeance, is the prescribed method of achieving victory. The young brave does not fail to follow this advice, and the pipes of the sand spirits are thus filled again with the magical substance which connects them to the Dream Worlds during those months of each year that they remain awake in the exterior world.

His spirit-wife is associated with the mystical Evening Star, the Abode of all Women, and it is this Venusian starlight that preserves the essential connection between the sand spirits, human consciousness, and the world of dreams. Another source states of this spirit-wife: 'She shall put on the beauty of the star-light, and become a shining bird of the air.'

It is difficult not to connect this story with the Sandman who comes to escort us to Dream Land, he who is also known throughout many mythologies as the Piper of Dreams ... the sandpiper. Why is sand connected with the divine dispensation to dream? A Gaelic poet once said that the man who goes to Tir-fo-Tuinn, the Land-Under-Wave where all dreams are fulfilled according to the measure of their dreamer's longing, enters into another world where the human soul is sand, and God is but the unloosened salt, the pure crystalline light of consciousness.

We might think, too, of the words of Eleanor Farjeon, the children's poet and storyteller who wrote the famous hymn, *Morning Has Broken*: 'Builders in silver-sand, dreamers in snow!'

Sand secretes within its particles certain necessary ingredients that the ancient alchemists needed to create a unique form of glass that contained the 'Spiritus Mundi', the 'breath of the universe' or the 'breath of the stars'. The glass contained a special quality of light which burst forth from these ingredients after particular sacred rhythms of heat, cooling, and attuned human breath, had been applied to them. The glass captured this light as an intrinsic quality, almost in the way that a magician's vial might capture a spirit, for the light was not of this Earth. This glass was placed as stained glass in the mighty cathedrals erected in the 12th century by the Knights Templar, who knew the secret method of producing it.

The light in the glass connects with certain centres in the human head, actually present within the brain as well as in ethereal existence, which can transport the soul into exalted worlds of the spirit even though it exists in a physical body upon the mundane sphere of Earth, akin to the sand spirits' pipes, which also involve breath, sacred natural ingredients, and ritual burning.

In other words, our God-given gift of dreaming and crafting ethereal images, upon which initial procedure everything we bring into existence depends – and therefore our life on Earth as human beings – is connected with sand. And sand is formed by the sea and the vast movement of the oceanic waves.

To understand better the profound message of the sandpiper, we need to turn again to the illustrious wisdom and insight of the Celtic poet and seer, Fiona Macleod, she who was connected at her very source and soul to the great ocean that rolled around the enchanted Western Isles of the Hebrides which she knew so well. The vision came to her on the shores of dream, the very domain of the sandpiper, those enchanted moments between sleeping and waking:

> It is less easy to interpret or accept (compared to meditative
> vision) either the rounded and complete dream of sleep –
> that rarity – or the waking dream that comes not less
> mysteriously unsought, clanless among the tribes of the
> day's thoughts, an exile from a forbidden land, a prince
> who will not be commanded in his going or coming, who
> knows not any law of ours but only his own law.

It is to write of one such vision that I took up my pen and have written these things. It was a dream in sleep, but so potent an image, that, with both body and mind alert in startled wakefulness, I saw it not less clearly, not less vividly, not less overwhelmingly clear and present. Its strangeness was in its living nearness in vision, and perhaps neither in aspect or relation may appeal to others. Perhaps, even, it will seem no more than a luminous phantasy, void of significance.

But, to me, it appeared, later, as an effort on the part of the spirit to complete in symbol what I had failed to do in words, while I have been writing these foregoing pages on the children of water – of those in whose hearts is the unresting wave, and whom the tides of happy life lift and leave, and whose longing is idle as foam, and whose dreams are as measureless as all the waters of the world.

I saw, suddenly, greenness come out of the sea, and then the sea pass like a dewdrop in the heat of the Sun. A vast figure stood on the bare understrand of ocean, and leaned on his right arm along a mountain-brow so high that it seemed to me Himalaya or the extreme Cordillera. As he leaned, I could not see the face, for the Titan stared beyond the rim of the world. But he leaned negligently, as though idly watching, idly waiting. There was nothing of him but was green water, fluent as the homeless wave yet held in unwavering columnar suspense. Not a limb but was moulded in strength and beauty, not a muscle of man's mortal body but was there: yet the white coral of the depths gleamed through the titanic feet sculptured as in green jade, and the floating brown weed of the perpetual tide cast a wavering shadow among the sculptured green ridges and valleys of that titanic head. But it was not an image I saw; it was not an image of life, but life. There was not an ocean withheld in that bended arm, in that lifted shoulder, which could not have yielded in flying wave and

soaring billow, or heaved with a slow mighty breath
sustaining navies and argosies as drifting shells. When
thought stirred behind the unseen brows, tides moved
within these columnar deeps; and I do not doubt that the
vast heart was a maelstrom where the inrush and outrush
of tempestuous surges made a throb that shook the coasts
of worlds beyond our own.

Looking on the greatness of this upbuilded sea, this
titanic statue of silence and water, I thought I beheld the
most ancient of the gods, the greatest of the gods. Suddenly
I heard breaths of music, and a sound as of a multitude of
swift feet around me and beyond. I turned. There was no-
one. But a low voice, that ran through me like fire, spoke.

'*Look, child of water, at your god.*'

Again I heard breaths of music rise, like thin spirals of
smoke, but I did not see whence they came.

While the music breathed, I saw the Titan stand back
from the rim of the world. His face slowly turned. But a
whiteness as of foam was against my eyes, and a sudden
intolerable fear bowed my head. When I looked again I saw
only an illimitable sea that reached from my feet, green as
grass: and on the west of the world the unloosened rains
and dews hung like a veil. The unseen one beside me
stooped, and lifted a wave, and threw it into my heart.

Then I knew that I was made of the kinship of Mânan,
and should never know peace, but should have the
homeless wave for my heart's brother, and the salt sea as
my cup to drink, and the wilderness of waters as the
symbol of all vain ungovernable longings and desires.

And I woke, still looking out of time into eternity,
and saw a Titan figure of living green water sculptured like
jade, with feet set in the bed of ancient oceans; leaning,
with averted face, on a mountain-brow, vast as Andes,
vast as Himalaya.

This infinitely beautiful prose-poem of the sea that Fiona Macleod has given us, holds the key to the heart of the mystery of the sandpiper. We are our dream, and our dream encompasses us. Even though she describes the great elemental ruler of water (and we are of course subject to all five of the elemental princes), the essence of water concerns us all, for we were born forth from the water like Moses, or Taliesin, who shares the same mythology, and the living waters are our deepest source. What we dream, we are, and without the surge and fall of dream within us, we are nothing.

The sandpiper takes us back to source, and counsels us to look upon the whole picture of the vast blue main of our life. If we want to change something, or lift ourselves to a new level, the sandpiper cries: 'Dream it! Dream it! Dream it!'

Scaup (see also DUCK)

The scaup bears the same augury as the duck, with the addition that it will be necessary to attend to the black, the white and the various shades of grey indicated in the purification process for your emotions. In this way, you will release the potential of the glorious colour spectrum that longs to balance your polarities and find evocative expression between them.

Scoter (Common) (see also DUCK)

The common scoter bears the same augury as the duck, with the exception that a wider interpretation ought to be given to the emotions involved, because those highlighted by the scoter's appearance are those which connect us to the whole of humanity and to the fate of the planet. The scoter is a whistler and a piper, and counsels us to purify our emotions so that they express lightness of heart, good cheer, bonhomie, and a readiness to dance buoyantly with life.

The evocative soul-music of its calls cries to us: 'It is time to dispense with isolation of self! Join the dance! Join the dance!'

Scoter (Surf) *(see also* DUCK)

The surf scoter bears the divine *ayin* (the 16th letter of the Hebrew alphabet whose sacred meaning is the single eye of God) on its vivid orange beak. Its augury is the same as that for the common scoter and the duck, except that in addition it foretells that you are to become a pupil of some sort; your sacred darkness is about to reveal the rich spoils within. Look at the huge 'pupil' within the eye on the scoter's bill, and you will understand its prophecy.

It also bears a beautiful white 'window' across its forehead, at the point of the third eye, indicating that your learning will penetrate deep within and bring expansion and enlightenment to this centre. It cries: 'Knock, and the door shall be opened!'

Scoter (Velvet) *(see also* DUCK)
(N. America: **White-Winged Scoter)**

This scoter's augury, although encompassing that of the duck in general, is more mystical, less outwardly jolly, than that of the common scoter. Both the male and the female bear a diamond-shaped white patch at the rear of the wing, and the female has two pale marks on her head, like soft beams of moonlight against her dark plumage.

The Moon is of great significance in this bird's augury. Magnetism, the secrets of the night, women's wisdom, ethereal beauty, the opening of the gates to fairyland; all are embraced in the prophecy of the velvet scoter. In the velvet darkness of the night, your vision will open onto fields of virgin light, scintillating with spiritual promise. Jewels of the Moon raining down on you in a soft shower of crystal delights are promised when this bird sails into your soul-sphere.

Moonstones, pearls, silver leaf, clear crystal quartz, snow quartz – all bear good influences for you at this time. Carry them, wear them, and scintillate with the soft secret joy of the Moon, which will light your way and make the darkness as nothing.

Seagull

The seagull is a symbol of the soul. It wings its wind-tossed way over the majestic unfathomable ocean, and gives voice to its urgent, passionate, lamenting cry. It brings us a message of breadth and depth, of far horizons and limitless space. It can dive into the great ocean of life and feed on the many and varied sources of nutriment therein, or it can ascend into the upper regions of the air and sail under the stars.

It is said that the souls of fishermen, and all those who love the sea, call to earthbound humanity through the haunting cry of the seagull once they have passed beyond the veil. The strangest of all the folk-stories about the seagull is that it covets human eyes. Around the Somerset coast, custom forbade the feeding of a seagull or ever to look into its eyes. If you were foolhardy enough to do so, the same bird would visit you when you were in the sea, either in a boat, clinging to driftwood waiting for rescue in the event of a calamity, or simply swimming, and steal your eyes, leaving you to drown in misery.

This grisly folklore can be interpreted much more beautifully by recognizing that the seagull calls to us to throw off our psychological shortsightedness and the habit of keeping our eyes fixed on the ground. It would absorb our eyes into the essence of its own free-ranging soul, and give our pedestrian vision a gift of the panoramic verities.

When the seagull comes to you, cast off all notions of limitation and pettiness, all that cramps, hinders and stultifies. Rise into the upper air with the gull, and observe the rolling ocean which is your life, and the possibilities and potential in it. Ride the wave and tread the air, and then let your spirit soar and dive and rejoice in aerobatics, as the seagull does. The seagull cries to you: 'Unfurl the great white sails of your soul to the spiced breezes blowing from the four corners of the magnificent Earth!'

Serin (see FINCH)

Seven Whistlers

'The Seven Whistlers' are seven angels in bird form who come to humankind to warn them of impending disaster, whether at sea, down the mines, in battle, or in any place of work or at home. The calamity is always serious, and, if the birds are heeded, it is said that it can be averted or avoided.

The Seven Whistlers are not seven in number, but appear as a numerous flock of birds. They can be distinguished by their frantic whirling and circling, and particularly by their desperate, repeated, plaintive cries. They are not gulls or crows, which have a harsh call (although, at a pinch, it is to be supposed that the Seven Whistlers would manifest through any kind of birds that they could summon) but are birds with a pronounced whistle in their note. They have been identified in the past as lapwings, finches, plovers, curlews, widgeon, whimbrels and fieldfares.

They are associated with the hounds of the soul, the hounds of darkness and light: according to which note the soul is sounding, one pack or other is attracted to it. When crying or calling under normal conditions, these wailing birds are speaking on many levels to the human soul. But at times of danger, they become the Seven Whistlers, who amass purely to alert those who might be saved, or whose shock might be less destructive if they are forewarned.

Three reports of the Seven Whistlers (they are legion) will serve as examples. A correspondent wrote to *Notes and Queries* (21 October 1871), reporting that on 6 September that year, when he was in Yorkshire, he had seen immense flocks of birds flying restlessly and crying loudly during a storm. He was informed by his servant that these were 'the Seven Whistlers', and that they were warning of approaching disaster, adding that the last time they had appeared was just before the terrible explosion of 1862 at Hartley colliery in Northumberland. On the following morning (7 September), word came to the contributor of a dreadful mine disaster at Wigan.

The 24 March edition of the *Leicester Chronicle* reported in 1855 that a miner had been asked a few days before why he was not working, to which he had replied that it was not only he who was off work, but all

THE ORACLE OF THE BIRDS

his comrades as well. The Seven Whistlers had been heard, and they regarded it as foolhardy to disregard the warning. He explained that on two previous occasions, the Seven Whistlers had appeared but had been ignored, and each time two lives had been lost. He added that the men calculated that it would be safe to return to work the next day, as long as the Whistlers were not heard again.

Finally, the folklore recorder R M Heanley told of how he was once on a trawler in Boston Deeps when the Seven Whistlers were heard keening and crying above the boat. The fishermen took up the trawl without hesitation and returned to the shore, explaining that calamity would surely overtake them if they ignored this direct warning from the spirits.

If the Seven Whistlers fly to you, they come either to sound a warning, or to open your heart to the deep mysteries of soul and universe. To ignore them is to endanger yourself and your destiny.

Shag (*see* CORMORANT)

Shearwater (All Types)

The shearwater comes to us bearing the wisdom of the crone. Although shearwaters are generally silent, reports confirm that feline growling sounds, shrieking, raucous calls, eerie howling, screaming, crowing, cackling and cooing can be heard issuing from their nest sites, sometimes in the deep of the night, or when they are feeding. A witches' Sabbath is not difficult to imagine under the influence of such a cacophony!

Yet this seabird of the open oceans brings a benign augury. It bids us go to the very root of things, to the source of ancient wisdom, to our ancestors themselves, for the enrichment of our lives and for the shedding of a most precious and unique light, new and yet steeped in antiquity, upon the questions and the seeking we hold at our core.

The crone is the queen and the keeper of such mysteries, and we can draw close to the heart of the crone shrouded in the essence of the shearwater by meditating upon this bird. We can hold, throughout, a natural object with which we associate great age – a stone, a crystal, a twig from an ancient tree (I have had great success with a piece of coal!) – or an item connected with our personal ancestors, in order to ritualize our meditation. Another method is to call on a mythological hero or heroine from our own culture before retreating within.

The shearwater carries in its name the idea of cutting the water. It slices through the ever changing, restless waves (outer manifestations of form) and delivers us to the bedrock beneath – our sacred roots.

Shelduck (also RUDDY SHELDUCK) (see DUCK)

Shoveler (see also DUCK)

This duck with its great heavy beak and highlights of powder blue on its wings lives on inland marshes, pools and lakes. It signifies reflective situations concerning the transformation and purification of emotions, as does all the duck family. In the case of the shoveler, we can think of its great beak filtering the surface water of its habitat via serrations along its edges to feed on tiny creatures overlooked by other water fowl. Its enormous bill is not used to 'shovel' down disproportionate amounts of food, but is rather the perfect tool for this subtle and refined feeding.

When the shoveler enters your soul-sphere, it comes as a fellow, to offer recognition that what you are currently experiencing in your life, or what might be a permanent aspect of your nature, is indeed a fine filtering of the waters of life so that you might nourish yourself on unsuspected aspects of it that others overlook.

The tool you use for this might be perhaps your emotions and your sensibilities, a certain way of viewing things, being different in some way, even a so-called 'hindrance' such as some kind of disfigurement or impediment which might manifest in many possible forms, such as poverty. And it may be that this is scoffed at or regarded as comical or undesirable by those around you. This is deplorable ignorance, of course, because when the shoveler takes flight, it rises on wings marked with azure blue – the blue of heaven. That which draws mockery or patronizing sympathy is the very tool that will craft your deepest happiness so that your wings unfurl and lift you into the highest heaven.

You are counselled not to turn back, not to be thrown off course or to be put off your stroke. The road you are travelling is the right one. The shoveler quacks quietly, wisely: 'Blue skies await!'

Shrike (Great Grey)

Very like a diminutive hawk, though not of the hawk family, the great grey shrike is in fact no larger than a blackbird, although it sports a hooked beak, hovers over and swoops on its prey, uses surprise tactics as hawks do, and has a harsh, screaming falcon-like call, sometimes also chattering like a magpie. It is an attractive, vividly marked bird, of pale grey-and-white plumage with black wings, tail and eye-stripe. When it presents itself to you as a spirit-bird, it will fix its beady eye on you with a shrewd candour. It has taken note of the black, the white, and the shades of grey in between.

It may be small, it may not be a hawk according to our classification, but it is certainly a ferocious bird of prey. It keeps what is called a 'larder', where, Bluebeard-like, its victims are stored, impaled on thorns. These hapless trophies usually consist of redpolls, siskins, and occasionally swallows; but sometimes even fieldfares, actually slightly larger than the shrike itself, have been discovered as components of this strange and ghoulish pantry.

The shrike is not a bird to mess with or to make light of! Its message (and who would dare to disregard it?) is that of course you are up to the task! Who cares if it may seem as though you lack the appropriate training or education, do not look the part, do not move in the right circles, have insufficient time, facilities, support? The shrike is not interested in excuses. You have it within you to succeed, and that ends the story.

The shrike calls – and none too softly – 'Engage in this challenge! You will win!'

Shrike (Red-Backed) (*see also* SHRIKE (GREAT GREY))

This smaller shrike bears a similar augury to that of the great grey shrike, except that it also brings a warning about unsuspected predatory tendencies in others. Someone with whom you come into close contact may have 'killer instincts' and may be targeting you or your work, or someone with vampiric tendencies may have attached themselves to you, draining your energies and motivation. It could be that someone is leading you astray, persuading you to engage in activities that you know are wrong, and yet you feel compelled to participate by the sway of their fascination or by the hypnotic force of their will.

This little bird, smaller than a starling, signals that you have the strength of character and the self-command necessary to throw off any or all of these influences and reclaim your power. Doing so will invigorate you and help you to release the dynamics within your personality that will express indomitable moral courage. The red-backed shrike counsels you not to be suspicious of others, but to be aware. It gives you its shrewd knowingness, and cries with its chattering shriek: 'You are invincible! Know it, and you will express it!'

Siskin (*see* FINCH)

Skua (All Types) (*see also* SEAGULL)
(N. America: Jaeger)

The skua is a very aggressive seabird, smaller than the herring gull (except for the great skua, which is about the same size). The skua has beautifully marked and shaped wing feathers, which change in pattern over the course of several years until it ultimately attains its adult plumage. There is a shamanic mystery about their changing design, as though they have flown out of the magical Otherworlds of soul initiation.

They are indeed the warriors of the seabird clan, attacking even cattle and humans fearlessly and ferociously to defend their nesting and feeding sites, and haranguing other birds into giving up their spoils.

149

When you need an injection of power and resolution from the spirit of the eternal warrior, the skua comes to help you and to initiate you, and to bless you in the undertaking of your challenge.

Occasionally it sounds a warning that your own aggression might be expressing itself harmfully. This bird, which 'mimics' raw belligerence so that we might learn how to overcome the negative traits of undisciplined force, will help you to channel your harmful aggression into a powerful protective instinct that will urge you to shield everyone from harm. This is the mark of the true warrior, who defends but does not attack. Hoodlums attack. The skua will help you to differentiate and marshal the energies of the warrior. Use its mighty, intrepid, ocean-faring forces!

Skylark (also Woodlark)

Lark means 'little song' and its collective noun is 'exaltation' (an exaltation of larks), which perfectly describes these exuberant choristers of the air. The skylark takes the Islamic 'straight path' right up into the heavens, often until it is invisible from the ground. As it does so it rains down a song so joyous and jubilant and golden that it is said to be the sound of happiness itself. This richly symbolic bird is a continuing source of inspiration to humanity. Its song signifies the river of creative joy which flows from the higher worlds to Earth when the earthbound soul breaks its chains and rises into the spiritual dimension whilst still inhabiting a physical body. It is Buddha attaining Nirvana, Krishna playing ecstatically on his flute; it is also a symbol of the Ascension of Christ.

The skylark is often the first bird to break the silence of the fading night at the first glimmering of dawn, and its song takes on, at such times, a poignant silvery tone, a strange sorrowful sweetness which is lost in cheerfulness as the morning progresses. The mellow, rapturous song of the woodlark is one of the most beautiful examples of birdsong on Earth, and to hear it is to be drawn deep into the heart of nature and on into the Otherworld, for their boundaries blur. For these reasons, the skylark is held as sacred in the Shetland Islands of Scotland. It is known as 'Our Lady's Hen' and anyone who harms it brings down three curses upon their own head.

The lark of sky and wood bids us go straight for the mark and says with Rumi: 'Dissolve your body in vision and ... pass into sight!'

Smew (see also DUCK and SEAGULL)

The augury brought by the smew is the same as that attaching to ducks generally, except that the snow-crested smew signifies royally exalted emotion, purified as if on snow-capped mountain heights. When our emotional depths become 'clear and pure as the sanctified mind of a devotee', we are usually ready to express the beauty of what our inner waters reflect through the medium of the arts. This is the message of the smew.

Sometimes smews attract a following of gulls as they feed, which are eager to share their meal. This circumstance adds further significance to their augury, because it combines with that of the seagull. The seagull urges on us unfettered vision, an expansion of the mind and the mind's horizon. The seagull's exhortations integrate with those of the smew, encouraging us to aspire to our highest art in any project we are undertaking.

Snipe

This secretive water bird, with its exceptionally long, thin beak and its strange drumming, made by its rigid tail-feathers in its downward flight during aerial displays, is a pointer bird. It is a keeper of the secrets of the lonely marshes and wetlands where it makes its home, and is particularly in touch with the poignant fairy life existing therein. Folklore tells us that its vivid stripes are a give-away sign that it is in touch with the fairies and is a guest at their revels.

The female is the dominant bird of the pair, and takes her pick of several males before finally settling down with one for the breeding season. A group of snipes on the ground are called a *walk*, incorporating the idea that they 'walk with the spirits'. A number of airborne snipes are called a *wisp*, perhaps originating from the fairy spirit called 'will-o'-the-wisp' which floats around in spheres of luminous marsh gas and which, in company with the snipe, is also a way-shower.

If the snipe flutters into your field of inner or outer vision, draw close to it in meditation, and visualize it clearly. Its extraordinarily long beak will point something out to you and will indicate the way forward, or else, after having consulted with the snipe, someone or something in your life will, unbidden, thereafter do the honours.

Snipe (Jack) (*see also* SNIPE)

The jack snipe is most definitely a fairy bird, richly steeped in the fair folk's magic and tradition. Although it bears a similar augury to the snipe, it is mainly a luck-bringer.

One of its favourite tricks during the breeding season is to make a sound like a cantering horse from its hidden dwelling-place in the marshlands, although its horse impressions are seldom heard by human ears as it nests in boggy, open areas of lonely sub-Arctic forests, and is a late summer and winter visitor only. Nevertheless, it is a luck-bird and a fairy bird, and brings its own little train of blessings.

Sparrow

The sparrow is a bird of Venus, deeply associated with the Goddess, the feminine principle of the Godhead, and as usual we see the poor little sparrow thoroughly abused in folklore because of it! Tales abound of all the horrible and unjust things it did to the male deity. When Christ was in the Garden of Gethsemane, all the other birds tried to confuse his pursuers, but the sparrows betrayed him by chirruping loudly in his vicinity! On Calvary, when the swallows stole away the executioners' nails, the sparrows pursued them and retrieved the nails! When Christ had been strung on the Cross, the tender-hearted swallows attempted to save him from further applied tortures by crying 'He is dead! He is dead!' only to be flatly contradicted by the sparrows, who cried 'He is alive! He is alive!' gleefully encouraging his tormentors to devise further cruelties!

Sparrows guard the Devil's fire, and chase away the swallows and robins who come to carry a portion of the flames to humanity for its blessing. If a sparrow is caught, it will kill its capturer by evil magic, and it is an omen of death if one flies into a house...and so the tales go on, getting wilder and wilder as they paint this cheerful, inoffensive little bird as a black-hearted villain who is very hostile and dangerous to the human population. It is even associated with human illness, the evidence presented being that when, in 1643, Major John Morgan lay desperately ill in the house of the father of the folk-historian John Aubrey, a sparrow came to the window of the sick-room every day and pecked at the lead of the same panel. It visited without fail until the Major had recovered sufficiently to vacate his bed and leave the house, whereupon the sparrow also took its leave and was never seen again.

That this factual story should be construed by folklorists as mystical proof that the sparrow brings illness to human beings is, as Pooh Bear might say, positively startling, for it seems obvious to me that the bird brought an angelic and spirit-link with that heavenly ray of healing which is focused on the heart to strengthen and restore it, an act of regenerative mercy of which Major Morgan's illness suggests he stood very much in need, as his condition took him to the brink of death. This association of the sparrow with the human heart is highly significant, as we shall see. John Clare, the poet, understood the connection, and had a tender fondness for the little sparrow he tamed and kept as a companion, deploring humanity's cruelty to this innocent bird.

One of the most telling legends from these later sources of folk-belief is that the sparrow's legs are fastened by invisible bonds, so that it can never run or walk, but only hop, and that its flesh is unclean and poisonous. As the sparrow's folk-history reads like one of the more extreme attacks by the Sunday tabloids, it is worth re-examining its mystical associations. With the dove and the swan, the sparrow is sacred to Venus. The royal swan is symbolical of our higher selves, whilst the dove signifies the love of the Holy Spirit; but it is the sparrow which, in folklore and in the Language of the Birds, is an emblem of human attachment, of the human love which sustains partnerships, families and communities.

Imperfect it may be, subject to disagreements and misunderstandings (the sparrow can be pugnacious) but one thing is certain; our human ability to love is divine, and ever struggles towards perfection; and it is

153

the one element, the one force, which can overcome the destructive dynamics of the aggressive, power-seeking ego, which grows so assertive and dangerous when it is not balanced by the feminine principle of the Godhead. As in the story of Venus overcoming the war-mongering Mars, so the Spirit of Love, the Goddess, turns humanity away from self-aggrandizement and the urge to dominate, by releasing and fostering the power of sweet human love, and in doing so bestows on humanity its saving grace.

That the sparrow expresses the essence of the soul is confirmed by the shamans of many tribal cultures who, when they enter the Otherworld to rescue a soul which has become lost in its wanderings, find it present there in the form of a sparrow.

I can again only encourage those who would believe the sparrow's bad press to read Claire Kipps' true account of the sparrow she rescued in her book, *Sold for a Farthing*, which describes how the little bird mirac-ulously inspired and nurtured human love. If we recognize Venus as a portrayal of the Great Goddess of All, then we see that the swan is the soul of Venus and the dove is her mystical heart; but the humble sparrows are the emanations from that ineffable heart, rising and falling in their thousandfold flocks among her exquisite robes, which are the holy outbreathing of her consciousness; and speeding at her command to quicken and bless the simple love in human hearts. And how foolish to try to denigrate this valiant little bird by means of Christ, who honoured women and loved the birds of the air!

When we see truly, we understand that the cheerful sparrow is a symbol of wholeheartedness, of the open, vibrant, tender heart-chakra – its regular, vigorous, musical chirping rather like the beat of a singing, love-attuned heart.

Sparrowhawk (*see also* HAWK and SPARROW)

The augury borne by the sparrowhawk is the same as that given for the hawk, with the addition that its appearance can sound a warning. The hawk is a symbol of the higher self, or the spirit, that most exalted point of our being that connects us to the Divine source.

When the sparrowhawk swoops on the sparrow, the symbol of the soul (the earthly sparrowhawk actually consumes quite a variety of small birds), we can see that what happens from a spiritual point of view is supremely right and follows a blessed and sunward course. The hawk is the hawk of godly love, pursuing the soul like Francis Thompson's Hounds of Love, promising a cosmic sunburst of consummation and initiation.

Yet the augury can have quite a different connotation. If the enquirer is in danger, if what is cruel and predatory lies in wait for her or him, then the sparrowhawk appears as a warning of that deadly bolt from the blue.

Your own finely-tuned intuition will reveal to you which augury it is. If it is a warning, you will perceive the sparrowhawk as a cold, stark, daunting presence, grey as death, manifesting as the Hawk of Winter. An event that marked the sparrowhawk as a bird of sacrifice in its winter guise, presaging the death of a king by surrendering its own life, occurred before the demise of Charles II. John Aubrey states in his *Miscellanies* (1695):

> Not long before the death of King Charles II a sparrow-
> hawk escaped from the Perch, and pitched on one of the
> Iron Crowns of the White Tower, and entangling its string
> in the Crown, hung by the heels and died. T'was
> considered very ominous, and so it proved.

Yet when this priests' falcon brings an augury that is warm and benign, the sparrowhawk will appear to your inner eye as almost golden in the heavens, its greyer plumage seeming like a soft summer mist that is sometimes present in the first early brightness of a shining dawn. When the sparrowhawk blesses, as in the latter case, your course is assured. If you reap the Hawk of Winter, however, you are counselled to stop and pause for a while before deciding on the road ahead.

Consult the oracle of the sparrow (above). Is your heart-attunement somehow off-key? Align your being with your deepest heart, and then walk on unafraid. Even if the predatory force strikes, you need not fear, as you will not be overthrown.

Spoonbill (*see also* HERON and WHITE HERON (LITTLE EGRET))

The heron-like spoonbill, a little larger than the white heron or little egret but smaller than the grey heron, wears a band of gold around its breast. It is associated with the Golden Mountain, to which reference is found in fairytale, myth and shamanic lore. For instance, Yakut shamans believe that the Pole Star, the 'white star of the north', is the 'navel of the sky' – a vast cosmic centre. They further believe that a central mountain joins heaven and Earth. The Pole Star is supposed to be fixed to the summit of this central peak, which is spoken of as a great golden mountain, visible only to the enlightened. The white and golden 'heron', the spoonbill, is the bird of the Golden Mountain, symbolizing it and the white Pole Star at its peak. From this northern star and the golden mountain which grounds its rays, the secret knowledge of God is said to flow to Earth.

The spoonbill, keeper of the sacred knowledge, stands guard as the divine heron over Sing-su-hay, a sanctified lake of Tibet, 'pure as pearls', which is famous for its exquisitely golden sands.

> Bright are the waters of Sing-su-hay,
>
> And the golden floods that thitherward stray...

wrote Thomas Moore in 'Paradise and the Peri'. If the spoonbill comes to us, we can in meditation see it standing in these beautiful waters, surrounded by sands of a brilliant ineffable gold, with the Golden Mountain radiant as visionary sunlight rising like an angel behind it, unearthly yet connected to the Earth.

East and west, the heron, in all its various incarnations, is keeper of the Bright Knowledge, the stream of enlightenment that shines from the Golden Mountain, from the northernmost star. With its great beak, the spoonbill counsels that you should never allow yourself to be spoon-fed by others regarding this most illustrious among wisdoms – the brilliance of your soul's inner eye – but reminds you that you can spoon-feed yourself heartily among its sublime harvest of flowers and diamonded dews. This harvest is gathered and ingested by meditation, contemplation, by drawing close to the spirit of beauty, by embracing and radiating love.

The telling of a traditional fairytale to illustrate the spoonbill's lesson might help to internalize it.

A queen had a daughter named Fair-Star, of peerless beauty. She was to be married to the noble King of the Mines of the Golden Mountain, and she looked forward with maidenly joy to her wedding day. She made a pilgrimage into the wilderness with her mother to consult with the Spirit of the Desert concerning her future, for the Spirit gave forth oracles.

But the Yellow Dwarf had secretly followed the two women, and put a spell on them to make them weary. They lay down to sleep before reaching the cave of the oracle, which was located at an oasis, and when they awoke they saw two mighty male lions approaching. The Yellow Dwarf appeared to the mother and daughter and promised to save them if Fair-Star would consent to be his bride. As the lions were about to devour her mother, Fair-Star was compelled to give her consent.

The Yellow Dwarf gave a strange musical call, and an orange-tree appeared and opened to them, into which they entered. They fled down a long stairway of brass until they came to a subterranean river of dark silver upon whose banks bobbed a little boat. They set sail in the boat, and fell asleep again. When they awoke, they were back home in their palace, but both had fallen sick.

Fair-Star's wedding-day approached, but still she languished. The King of the Golden Mines was insistent that she should be his bride, however; but on her wedding-morning the Yellow Dwarf appeared and carried her off to his home, called Steel-Heart Castle.

Meanwhile, the Spirit of the Desert held the King of the Golden Mines captive, so that he was unable to escape from the desert. Here he wandered desolately until one evening he came to the shores of a wide and rolling indigo sea. A mermaid rose up from the midnight-blue waves and bore him in her arms to Steel-Heart Castle. Here she gave him a wondrous sword that had been miraculously crafted from a single diamond. He entered the castle and with his blade of marvels he successfully overcame four hostile sphinxes, six wrathful dragons and twenty-four cannibalistic nymphs. All these he slew with the virgin sword of pristine light, until at last he came to the princess' chamber, where she awaited him.

Thinking he had completed his mission, he dropped his sword. But the Yellow Dwarf was waiting, and immediately availed himself of it. He took the king captive, asking him to relinquish Fair-Star forever. The king refused, at which the Yellow Dwarf drove the diamond sword through his heart. Seeing him fall, Fair-Star threw herself upon his dying body and perished.

Far away in her white palace, Fair-Star's mother read her daughter's fate in the ethers, and entered into the service of the Spirit of the Desert, remaining in mourning for the rest of her life.

This tragic fairytale shows us Fair-Star as the soul seeking knowledge of the Pole Star and consummation with the Golden Mountain, and the king as the soul seeking knowledge of the Golden Mountain and consummation with the Pole Star. (*See* Appendix 2.)

The importance of the spoonbill's message cannot be underestimated. Reject dogma, indoctrination, and the temptation to let others do your ethical and spiritual thinking for you. If you are fettered at this level of life, you are likely to become both a brutalized and emasculated prisoner indeed.

Starling

King Charles II kept a caged starling in his bedchamber. This tame, talking bird of royal favour was afterwards presented to the great diarist Samuel Pepys, who continued to keep it as a pet. The handsome starling seems to share an affinity with human beings, and easily learns to mimic our speech. Human-like, it walks rather than hops. It is a bird that travels in flocks, amassing in great numbers in towns and cities as well as the countryside. It derives its name from the medieval root 'staer' (old German for 'star'), and as a child I was fascinated with its night-sky plumage, which shines in the spring with tiny purple, white, bronze and green stars scintillating on a background of glossy midnight-black feathers.

The starling signifies community, integrity, communal living and singleness of purpose. Its chattering cacophony, eccentrically musical, contains within it many sounds that are reminiscent of machinery: the cogs and wheels of the industry of social structure, networking, social integration and statecraft. Starlings suggest the vast organized powers of State, society, Church, judiciary. They bring inspiration as to how to survive within these all-encompassing frameworks without losing our sense of individual empowerment and choice. We can work as a team and experience singleness of purpose, and then bring that same experience to bear in our own personal lives. We can function in one sense as an atom of the limb of Leviathan, and yet still retain our unique integrity.

The awe-inspiring flights of multitudinous starlings flocking together are one of the great wonders of nature. They demonstrate that we do not lose our individual spiritual connection to the Divine by merging and fusing with one another, but rather give it greater, one-pointed, mystical expression than we would otherwise be unable to achieve.

The poet Coleridge saw in them the extremes of the soul in its subconscious state wrought into pictures: 'Pain...or fantastic Pleasure that draws the Soul along swimming through the air in many shapes, even as a Flight of Starlings in a Wind.' The language of the Unseen speaks through these great flights of starlings – a soul-empowering language of heaven that would never be able to manifest in the outer world without the individual dedication of each bird to the wondrous whole.

The starling chatters: 'The dewdrop slips into the sea, but the dewdrop can always re-emerge, stamped with the impress of the whole magnitude of the surging ocean.'

Stilt (Black-Winged)

The black-winged stilt signifies the grace, beauty and calm that come to the soul when it directs its perspective away from the ground. It is not a mountain-bird, yet it urges us to seek the mountain-tops in our meditations and in our imagination so that it will seem as if we are always drawing on their pure and stimulating airs and watching our lives and the world from their free and airy vantage-point.

The stilt, with its extraordinarily long and slender roseate legs, makes its home on sequestered lakes and shallow coastal lagoons. Its message concerns the still, reflective qualities of the soul, which manifest when the harsh jangling and reactionary irritations of the lower mind are brought into harmony and peace by the command of the spiritual will. This guiding force of the soul becomes strong through meditation, contemplation, intuitive rendering of the Bright Knowledge (whose wisdom the soul knows in its depths), embracing the spirit of beauty and, most significant of all, the expression of love at every level of life.

Like the swan and the duck, the stilt is a bird of the Lady of the Lake, who hands to us all the sword of truth and soul-nobility to wield throughout our lives. If you use the lake as a meditative symbol, the stilt will gracefully usher you into her domain, which is timeless, marvellous and transcendental.

When the stilt comes to you, it shows you the sanctuary of peace within, and affirms that you can find it and draw on it and live within its enchanted environs even while you live your practical, everyday life.

Stonechat

The stonechat is another little 'live-wire' bird. Smaller than a robin, the male has a black head with white neck patches and a reddish-and-white breast, whilst the breast-feathers of the female are paler, and her back, wings and head are sparrow-like.

The stonechat lives on lowland heaths and among gorse bushes near the sea, but it also inhabits golf courses and railway embankments.

Its nervous, twitching, darting habits and the fire on its breast alert us to its augural significance regarding the senses. In the case of the stonechat, it brings our attention to our ears. The sense of hearing, both at the inner and the outer level, is what the stonechat emphasizes. It urges us to safeguard our hearing, and to begin to really listen; listen to the sounds of the natural world, listen to the tones and rhythms of music, listen to those who engage us in conversation, and listen within the silence of our own being.

It bids us consider how our attitudes, prejudices and mind-sets can make our hearing extremely selective, and to begin to recognize our range of self-imposed deafness. When the stonechat comes to us, we will be given a valuable gift of realization through our hearing if we open our ears and remain alert. Heart-centred listening – understanding what is really being conveyed through the speech of others and listening intently to our inner guidance, our intuition – is a vital part of the art of listening.

The physical and spiritual health and function of the ears is the concern of this little bird's augury, expressed in its song-flights and in its call, which sounds like two pebbles being knocked together. This explosive little sound, like the clappers in unresonant bells, cries: 'Those with ears, let them hear!'

Stone Curlew

This strange nocturnal bird with its weird haunting cry is among the lamenting clan which comprises the Seven Whistlers (*see entry*). The stone curlew is a bird of barren stony ground, arid pastureland, sand dunes, heath and desert. In Britain it occupies chalk downs, sparsely covered arable land and the desolate stretches of old airfields. Its plaintive cry begins at dusk and continues through the watches of the night. Its head, body and tail are a sandy buff colour, but its wings are black flecked with white, like glancing moonlight.

This bird expresses the colour yellow. Its yellow eyes are large, striking and hypnotically staring. Its long legs are yellow. Its bill, tipped with black, is yellow. It intimates sorrow, haunting, desolation and lamentation. Yet the poignancy of these mourning inscapes brings promise of a roseate, rising joy even keener than the sorrow it will eventually supplant. Sorrow scoops a receptacle in the previously unsculpted levels of the soul that this promised joy will fill.

The sorrow of the stone curlew arises from the condition of the mind of man as it broadcasts throughout our world, throughout the cosmos. Yellow is the colour of the mind, and as one of the seven rays of creation its proper manifestation is brilliant, deep, and of a shining, joyful pulchritude. The weird yellow in the staring eye of the stone curlew shows us a sickness in the mind of man, a haunted suspension of the free and God-ward energy flow that should course through that collective mind in countless configurations creative of joy, liberty and fullness of vision upon planet Earth. And yet it stares, hypnotized, in sick yellow. This, the stone curlew knows and conveys, and as a bird of arid, stony places it is showing us that where the mind's flow is blocked is at the point of the heart, through which it has forgotten how to flow. This brings a peculiar deadness and lethargy to its ability to respond with healing solutions to the huge issues and crises of our time, and a tendency to pursue supposedly antedotal routes that actually make the original problem worse, simply because it has cut itself off from its supply of real intelligence, which is the all-seeing eye in the heart.

The staring deadlocked eye of the wilfully dispossessed mind should even convey to the preening intellect, so exasperatingly assured of its own deified status and which in our sick and mesmerized state we worship as an idol, that something is wrong, that its own conception of reality is somehow not quite measuring up. Something is hypnotizing us.

The augury of the stone curlew is that we would do well to review a tendency to depend on the intellect, on the conceits of the mind, in forming our judgments. Too much credence is being given to its blinkered analyses. We need a deeper, all-encompassing perspective that can only be found in the sanctity and stillness of the heart. The focus of the mind alone can all too often bring obsession, compulsion and distortion in its wake, as when we concentrate with the mind on a sickness, pain or fear, and find that it becomes magnified.

To find the magic in the heart, gently hold in meditative vision the perfect form of a rose, blush-pink as with the soft benign fires of a sunrise sky. Breathe in its pure fragrance. Looking deep into its heart, you will find your own. This is the lesson of the stone curlew.

Although it teaches us about a sorrowful truth, the stone curlew is a beautiful, poignant, evocative bird filled with the spirit of wisdom. Its night wings reflect the redeeming moonlight. We shall come out of the defile it reveals to us. All will be well, even on the grandest of scales.

Stork (White) (see also HERON, SPOONBILL and EGRET (LITTLE))

This massive heron, a rare visitor to Britain, denotes fertility, abundance, happy outcomes, the wisdom of Goddess and sexual magic in the simple and human sense as well as that of the esoteric. Such is its gladdening message. It also signifies the delight we take in babies and all young, growing things. There is a pure radiance, an emanation of the spirit, in newborns which is unique. It beams in tiny soft-sparkling star formations off their aura, which is entirely fresh and undefiled.

The stork advises the exercise of imagining ourselves born from the sea, the great mother, new and fresh in the first morning light, whenever we feel jaded and disenchanted with life. Just rise newborn from the heart of the ocean and embrace the dawn (whatever the time of day!). In this way, we can keep in touch with the joy of stork magic.

Swallow

One of the four birds that brought fire to humankind (its companions being the wren, the lark and the robin) thereby gaining its red markings and its smoky blue feathers, the swallow is regarded as a bird of blessing in many cultures. Its sister is said to be the NIGHTINGALE, the gods bestowing on her the gift of beautiful song, and on her sibling the swallow the gift of becoming the renowned herald of summer.

The swallow is associated with water, and if it builds its nest on a house will protect the building from fire and lightning. If the swallows fail to return the following year to nest again, the house is considered to have lost its luck. Country people said that it knew where foul deeds had been wrought, and that it would never nest on a house where cruelty was practised. To disturb or, even worse, destroy the sacred swallow's nest was to invite calamity on one's own head.

The folk-custom collector Henderson recorded how, when a Hull banker purchased a farm, his sons removed all the swallows' nests from the eaves. 'The bank broke soon after,' Henderson was told, 'and, poor things, the family has had naught but trouble since.'

It is related by John Aubrey in his *Miscellanies* (1695) that during the time when Charles I was a prisoner, a wonder occurred when the Rector of Stretton in Herefordshire stood in the bay-window of his Manor House to drink to the king's health and longevity. As he raised the cup, a swallow appeared through the open window, settling on the vessel's brim. It drank a few drops of the cider before flying away. This has in retrospect been interpreted as a death omen; but in fact the swallow is the Bird of Returning and exists to remind us that summer will come again after the harshness of winter, for monarchs as well as the populace.

This incident links the bird with the far-seeing prophecy and psychic powers it is said to command, and with sight and vision. This gift of keen sight they were fabled to protect with the aid of the herb swallowwort (greater celandine), giving it to their young to clear the film that caused dim vision from their eyes.

The swallow also made use of a magical stone secreted within its body. This sought-after stone was considered to contain many healing virtues, and its properties included bestowing eloquence and acting as a love potion on a desired woman. The swallow was said to bring the stone from the shores of the sea, where it had been cast up by the mysterious Spirit of the Waves as a gift to the sacred summer bird of magic, healing and the powers of the psyche.

This connection with the gods and goddesses of the ocean wave reveals the swallow as the bird of the Divine Imagination, that miraculous power which gives life and form to all things. Ancient people spoke of two stones, one of black obsidian or jet, which contained the properties mentioned above, and another stone of red jasper or ruby, which cured insanity.

When the swallow comes to you, it signals the return of summer to your life, or seeks perhaps to remind you that summer will come again although you may be struggling through a period of darkness. It heralds the re-institution of good things, good feelings, happy situations, valued relationships, that you may have thought had passed forever from your life. It brings to you the creative power of the Divine Imagination, so that you can bring forth the artist, the creator within you, a magic which can be wrought to bless aspirations either humble or daring in scope.

It may come to bring you a message from the angels, from your guide, from a friend separate from you on either side of the veil, or from the Godhead itself. It may come to bring you that sacred spark of the Secret Fire which will inspire you to develop the powers of your spirit and your psyche. Its presence may foretell the advent of a voyage or a journey, on whatever plane, for the swallow signifies the Soul of the Wanderer, she or he who longs to search and seek and make discoveries.

The swallow is above all the holy arrow of desire, a sigil of the mysterious potential which can be fired from the heart into the heavens, sure to hit its mark and bring down to the Earth a treasure beyond price from the supernal worlds. This identification with a spirit-arrow goes hand in hand with the martin, which is seen as the divine bow, as in the old wise saw 'The martin and the swallow / Are God's Bow and Arrow'.

It will come as comforter or bird of joy, bringing to us either a reminder of the law which is ever-returning summer, or summer's essence in spiritual principle.

Swan

This exquisite bird, said to have a human soul, is the creature of a myriad myths. If there were not swans, we would surely call them forth from the imaginal world, for our spirit would need to envisage their grace, their dignity, the enchantment of their beauty, as we need to envisage the unicorn for its similar qualities. Swans on the water contemplating their reflection can seem to the onlooker as if they are birds of half vision and half dream, and the aura of their legend can often seem almost palpable.

In Scandinavian myth, the swan was the bird of the benign god Freyr and was associated with the white cirrus clouds, the clouds of fair weather, which formed his chariot. It was also the bird of valediction, the term 'swansong' being familiar around the world. The Valkyries were swan-maidens who flew before those they favoured in battle, summoning the souls of the slain to Valhalla.

In ancient Greece, Apollo's chariot was drawn by swans when he rode north to the land of everlasting youth. Apollo himself was fathered by a swan, together with his twin sister Artemis, for Zeus had impregnated their mother Leto in the shape of a great swan. This story reflects another, that of Leda, who was courted by the god Jupiter in swan form. Two eggs came forth from this union, one of them producing Castor and Pollux, the Heavenly Twins, whilst from the other sprang the mythical women Helena and Clytemnestra.

One persistent and widespread legend is that of the swan-maiden, which tells how some amorous swain secretly watches whilst a flock of swans leave their garment of feathers by the side of a woodland pool and bathe in the waters in the form of beautiful maidens. The young man, usually of humble origin, falls in love with one of the maidens and, careful to note which is her feathered garment on the next occasion that the swans assemble at the pool, steals it away. The swan is thereby trapped in her woman's body, and agrees to marry her suitor. She invariably finds her swan-feather garment at some point in the future, usually when she has given birth to several children, and leaves her husband without hesitation, leaving him to remember her, love-struck forever, through the unearthly gifts of music, song, poetry and dance that have been bestowed on her children.

The secret of this undying myth seems to be that the swan's spirit, or guardian fairy, is of such advanced and beautiful evolution that the bird and the spirit often merge and become one. The guardian spirit is seduced by the lure of human love away from its true destiny, until it is reminded by the earthly manifestation of the swan and returns again to its angelic task, which is concerned with both the bird's physical and soul evolution.

As the swan is so deeply associated with Zeus and Jupiter, gods of the thunderbolt or of the dynamic spark of life which forges creation itself, its eggs (which in legend produced so many mythical beings) were said to hatch only in thunderstorms, when the transforming kiss of the lightning would shatter the shell and bring forth the wonder within. The swan is also sacred to Aphrodite, Orpheus and Venus. Its purity is a Christian symbol of Saint Hugh of Lincoln and Saint Cuthbert. Buddha was moved to begin his teachings after rescuing a wounded swan, and the northern constellation Cygnus, the Swan, was placed in the sky by the gods to remind humanity of the northward-lying land of everlasting youth.

In Celtic legend, the beautiful queen Yewberry changes into a swan every other year at the time of Samhain, the Celtic New Year, and Oenghus, the god of love, transforms himself into a swan to woo her. The White Swans of the Wilderness were four children of the Tuatha De Danaan, an ancient magical race linked with the noble fairies. They were turned into swans by their jealous stepmother, and cursed to remain in swan form for 900 years, until Saint Patrick released them after Ireland had become Christianized. Until that time, they roamed the skies and the wild waterways, singing songs of beauty and melancholy with human voices.

The swan is said to sing, once, preceding death, although as a bird of the Threshold, she inhabits the inner and outer worlds, ever entering and leaving the spiritual realms through the Sacred Gate which is the mystic link between the two and is often associated with mist or twilight, both of which are symbolized by the swan; and so she sings not only on her 'death', those times when she enters the Otherworld, but also on her emergence from it. One old story tells that when a great company of swans wearing silver chains and golden coronets alighted on Lough Bel Dragon, they sang with such ethereal sweetness that all who heard them fell into an enchanted dream for three days and three nights. Nevertheless, their mellifluous death-song was mentioned by Plato and Aristotle, the latter claiming that it was often heard by sailors along the Libyan coast, who wept to hear its melancholic strains.

When the swan sings at the time of her death, it is said that she does so because her spirit is enraptured by her vision of the heaven-worlds which she is approaching; and when she sings at other times, it is because she is bringing the sublime sweetness of those worlds back to the Earth with her as she once again crosses the threshold between the supernal and the mundane.

The swan comes to you to bring you inspiration, especially if you are composing a song, a piece of music, a poem or a story; the swan's skin and feathers were used in druidic times to make the cloak that was presented to the bard as a signature of his high office. Sometimes the swan appears in order to beautify and bless a farewell, or to indicate that the time is right to make one. She is also the herald of the benediction of love and beauty preparing to come into a life, and as a symbol of the soul she bestows those graceful qualities belonging to it which are to do with love, reflection and depth, dignity and beauty, purity and stillness, solitude and self-discovery.

When the swan glides towards you, you are being asked to make a polished mirror of your soul so that you may reflect the spiritual worlds; for the swan is the great ensouler, and will help us to build the swift magical chariot that the spirit rides in and drives, which is truly the soul-essence.

Swift

The swift is a sacred and luck-bringing bird, sharing much in common with the swallow. Its cries are the exultation of the soul in the magical world of golden, slow-dwindling summer evenings. A wise saw which belongs to the swallow also includes the swift:

> The Robin and the Wren
>
> Are God Almighty's cock and hen.
>
> The Swallow and the Swift
>
> Are God Almighty's gift.

The swift brings the message of spiritual opportunity. These opportunities exist in abundance around us all the time, but typically we tend to miss most of them. The wise swift, who knows the mystical Source of all our strength and happiness, cries with the poet Amiel: 'Life passes swiftly, and we have not too much time for gladdening the hearts of those who travel the winding way with us. Oh, be swift to love! Make haste to be kind!'

Teal (see also DUCK)

The teal signifies that we need to purify our emotional and instinctive selves in preparation to receive some form of higher knowledge. This little duck bears a 'serpent's head', which is actually a green eye-patch that, fully incorporating the eye, is in the shape of a snake-head. Its golden tail reinforces the serpent symbolism, for the Serpent of the Higher Wisdom or the Serpent of Knowledge, significantly emerald-headed in this case, always bears some component of gold.

The sign of the teachings of the Druids was a golden serpent. The reference is to the Serpent-People, spoken of in ancient Sumer, who appear to be, according to many texts of remotest antiquity, our distant ancestors and who initiated humankind into the arts and sciences, including medicine, philosophy, technology and agriculture.

In ancient Egypt, the emerald was a sign of sanctified knowledge, and was particularly associated with the sacral and brow chakras (the 'third eye' and the sexual centre). It was associated with the Emerald Tablet, the Table of Destinies, which was said to contain all the divine knowledge that could ever be known on Earth. (See Appendix 1.) Whatever knowledge you are about to receive, whether it is deeply personal or spiritual in nature, or even if it seems concerned only with worldly affairs, such as training or promotion at work, will keenly impact your perception and the development of your soul. You will build it into the architecture of your deeper self and keep it forever.

The piping call of the teal as it twists and turns in its serpentine flight whistles: 'Make ready! Make ready! The halls of learning are calling you!'

Tern (All Types) *(see also* SEAGULL)

The tern bears a similar augury to the seagull, except that this assertive, sometimes aggressive seabird also signifies that you are being called on to develop warrior-like qualities. The tern's aggression is defensive, although it does occasionally enter into battle in order to win spoils from other sea-faring birds. This is the negative side of the warrior nature, which the tern actually warns against.

The tern foretells that adventure, scintillating challenge, new horizons, are about to appear in your life, and it urges you to be bold, intrepid, fearless and inwardly invincible, ready to draw freely on qualities associated with the legendary knight, the Indian brave, the voyaging adventurer, to help you in your quest. Its wild, rousing scream cries: 'You are about to come into your own!'

Thrush

The thrush, one of Britain's loveliest songsters, is the bird of the shaman. Its dappled breast and full-throated warbling are intimations of the Otherworld, and thrush-power or medicine can be learned by observing its habits. 'The early bird catches the worm' was surely a saying devised after watching the thrush assess with deadly sensitivity the exact location of an earthworm, and then yank it from its hole with unrelenting determination.

The message of the thrush is that we must marry beauty and spirituality with earthly efficiency and effectiveness, or else the gifts of the soul will lack the necessary nourishment of practical expression, and no proper receptacle can be forged to contain them.

Tit (*see also* BLUE TIT)

The tit is always a messenger of happy tidings. The general augury is given in the entry under blue tit. This overall auspice can be applied to the following types and their individual auguries:

Bearded Tit: happiness will come from an ancient source, such as associations with venerable and historical figures and their works, ancient systems of knowledge and wisdom, older people, old sites and buildings.

Blue Tit: *see entry*

Coal Tit: this little bird represents an obscured happiness, involving the heart, which will make itself known.

Crested Tit: the crested tit foretells an outstanding and royal visitation of happiness.

Great Tit: *see entry for* blue tit.

Long-tailed Tit: this tiny, charming little bird foretells the coming of happiness after a long and weary wait for its arrival. It is the signature of hope.

Marsh Tit: the marsh tit prognosticates the steady flow of calm and stable happiness after much emotional turmoil and distress.

Willow Tit: the willow tit predicts the birth of a deep, poignantly sweet happiness after great sorrow.

Tree Creeper

The valiant tree creeper, hardly bigger than a blue tit, looks almost like a wood mouse as it scurries up tree trunks, taking a spiralling path as it swiftly probes the bark in search of insects and grubs. Its long, slender, downward-curving bill and its straight, stiff pointed tail feathers give this little bird its distinctive features, however, as do its wings. When spread in flight, they look like the majestically-patterned wings of a large moth, barred, striped and mottled in buff and brown. It never pauses until it is almost at the top of the tree. When it has reached its goal, it flies to the next tree and begins again. It never descends the tree, and it never looks down.

This little dynamo brings us the message that, likewise, we should never look down, and that we should look back only with caution. Ruminative thoughts, dwelling on sadness and discouragement, can drain us of motivation and volition. The tree creeper sets a goal, embraces it, and then sets another one. It has no time for lethargy. Weariness and depression can be avoided if we refuse to take out the self-flagellating whips that lurk in our sad memories and regrets and which proffer themselves all too readily as we begin to lose momentum.

Although it is a frenetic little bird, the tree creeper shows us mandala-like, shamanic patterns when it spreads its wings. It is centred in the peace of the Otherworld. It urges us to take the time to meditate, because in meditation we control our thoughts and correct any drift towards a negative thought-path.

The busy, cheerful tree creeper also bids us think about spirits. It is very much in touch with the spirit of the tree as it embarks on each of its upward journeys from bole to leafy boughs. At night it loves to roost in a little crevice within the bark, marking such niches as its chambers. Choose a tree to which you are drawn, and learn about it. Learn its folklore and its healing properties, and ask the tree to be your guardian. Appoint it as your meditative symbol. There is no better way to root your thought-life into the good earth, and grow upwards in freedom, away from the heaviness and restrictions of everyday life. The little tree creeper, which resembles an animal and an insect and yet is a bird, lives out this example for us, and brings us an augury of healing. Its repetitive little call cries: 'Look up! Look up! Look up!'

Turnstone

This sturdy wader, black-and-white with orange wings in its summer plumage, loves to dodge the rippling waves and fling aside seaweed, small pebbles and shells in its search for food. It is active, going about its business with great determination and energy, and its message is clear. It comes to us when we need an injection of renewed vigour, focus and singleness of purpose. If we are feeling jaded and disheartened about a certain project or aim we have been trying to fulfil, it urges us to leave no stone unturned, no path uncleared, in pursuit of our aim.

With its ebullient mien it reminds us that we have the power-surge of the wide, rolling, ever-creative ocean to call on for replenishment, because the ocean exists within the worlds of the psyche as well as without. It calls with its twittering, metallic cry: 'Don't give up! Never give up! One more push will win the day!'

Twite (see FINCH)

Wagtail (All Types)

This appealing little bird is of prime importance in Japanese mythology, because it is the Bird of Life.

> When Izanagi and Izanami, the Divine Couple, stood upon the floating bridge of heaven in the earliest days of the world, with instructions to create the islands of Japan from their masters in the world of light, Izanagi dipped his jewelled spear into the waters of the primeval ocean whilst Izanami uttered incantations. Upon the surface of the waters the Earth sailed in a formless mass like a body of oil. But as they watched from their bridge, which was composed of dense cosmic clouds, they saw the waters begin to thicken and assume shape around the point of the jewelled spear. When Izanagi lifted it out of the imbroglio, a drop of the thickening waters suspended on its tip

solidified to form Onogoro, the very first island, whose name means 'spontaneously coagulated'.

Down the seven-tiered staircase of the rainbow came Izanagi and Izanami. They built a sacred pillar (called a *shem* in earliest Mesopotamian mythology, its function that of conveying the gods from heaven to Earth and back again, as the need arose) and beside it a wondrous palace which reflected the celestial worlds from which they had descended. Now that they occupied earthly bodies, they wished to physically consummate their love and have children, but they did not understand their separated material bodies (they had been as one in the heaven worlds) or what to do with them.

A pair of wagtails approached and, with the movement of their tails and by engaging in the act of mating, they showed the couple how to procreate. From this tutelary blessing bestowed by the wagtail came forth not only the remaining islands of Japan and all the lands upon the Earth, but the four elements and their various deities, followed by the human race and civilization, although Izanami died in giving birth to the elemental god of fire.

This idea of the wagtail as the primordial bird, which in its pairing reflected the Divine Couple and helped them to give forth life, echoes the notion that birds in their essence are of the great angelic stream of being. They contain the alpha and omega of creation because they are of the serpent (alpha or originating) race, as their claws and scaly legs indicate, and yet their destiny and their true expression of being is as free, winged, song-exuding denizens of the boundless skies (omega or fulfilment).

The wagtail embraces the theme of the eagle in that it is the keeper of the secret of life, which is that the King of the Air, the mighty eagle, will bear away the serpent in its talons and carry it to the highest heights because the serpent and the eagle are one. The gift of the bird is the gift of ascension. The gift of the serpent is the living essence of wisdom, the God-spark within the soul of the bird that urges it to take flight. When the wagtail comes to you, it comes to announce that you have within you the divine secret that initiates. The knowledge is intrinsically yours. You need only have faith in your inviolable containment of it, and connect with your heart-centre in meditation, to unlock it.

The secret of mastering your life – the serpent-wisdom – lies within you, and your destiny is ascension. The wagtail imparts these eternal verities with a friendly, pragmatic waddle, because its secret encompasses both the Earth and the heavens, knowing that they are one, and ever cry out for one another until they achieve union.

The wagtail whistles with its sharp, sweet call: 'Aim for the highest mark, but love and delight in the little, simple things of life with just as deep and great an aspiration!'

Warbler (All Types)

A particular and poignant story is told of this bird.

> In the earliest days of Christianity, a saint led a brotherhood of monks into a wood to establish a settlement there. They built their little wattle-and-daub cells, and the community flourished.
>
> One day, the saint went out into the wood to collect firewood, and as he stooped to tie his bundle, he caught sight of a little bird on a branch nearby which began to sing. The saint was so entranced by the beauty and purity of the warbler's song that he stood listening until it fell silent, his heart pierced by the poignancy of its cascading notes. When he carried the firewood back to the commune, he thought his eyes must deceive him, for everything had changed. Where the humble cells had once clustered stood a huge, beautifully constructed stone abbey with extensive grounds.
>
> A monk coming towards him asked him who he was. When the wondering saint told him, the monk exclaimed in

astonishment and ran back to the abbey, crying 'Saint
Malachi is found!' He was informed by the brethren that a
sacred story concerning the genesis of the brotherhood was
that their founder, Saint Malachi, had one day disappeared
into the woods, never to return, and it was afterwards
believed that an angel had taken him up into heaven.

The story had been preserved among them for seven
hundred years from the date of the saint's disappearance.
And a monk of Hildesheim, who was famous among his
colleagues for doubting how with God a thousand years
could be as a single day, also listened to the singing of a bird
in a wood for the duration of what he thought was three
minutes, only to find that in fact the time had stretched
across a span of 300 years.

Longfellow in 'The Golden Legend' tells of a milk-white bird who sang
to a monk called Felix for 1,000 years which seemed to him 'but a single
hour', so enchanted was he with its sweet liquefaction of song. All over
the world these legends exist, their common factor always being that the
enthralled listener aspired towards the heaven worlds, being a monk or
some other form of devotee.

And a tale is told of the Hyperboreans, the magical people of the far
north who were blessed by the Pole Star but who were always spoken
of as human, just as we are. This tribe of the extreme north, who dwelt
beyond Boreas (the seat of the north wind) which according to Virgil
was located under the North Pole, were said to be the oldest of the
human race, the most virtuous, and the happiest. It was rumoured that
they lived out life spans of over 1,000 years under cloudless blue
heavens, in fields yielding double harvests, and in the enjoyment of
perpetual spring. They danced with the spirits of the Northern Lights to
energize themselves with magnetic energy. When sated of life they
would crown their heads with chaplets of flowers and plunge headlong
from the mountain Halleberg into the sea, whereupon, without suffering
the pains of death, they would immediately be taken into the bosom of
the northern paradise, the Land of the Ever-Young. The point about the

Hyperboreans is that they did not live in an atmosphere like our own, but in a rarefied air whose particles resembled visible feathers.

Both Pliny and Herodotus report on this strange marvel, which they say must have been suggested by the quantity of feathery snow that falls in the arctic regions, even though the Hyperboreans in their living Eden were clearly never visited by snow, except as a white cap for their farthest mountain-tops.

The paradise of the north was rather a region of birds, not in a physical but a mystical sense, where it seems as if the spiritual atoms themselves were encoded with patterns relating to the light-seeds of ethereal bird life. Like the eagle, which in myth plunges into the sea or the waters of a sacred lake once every 500 years to renew its life-forces, and from which watery abyss it grasps the legendary serpent (the veritable symbol of those life-forces) in order to rise again, so the Hyperboreans flung themselves into the ocean deeps when their inner spark began to wane. And it was to this Hyperborean region, through the gates of Paradise, that the singing birds transported their enthralled listeners.

When the warbler, the bird of beautiful song, comes to you, you are being offered entry to paradise – not a false garden of delights where the ego dwells in monarchic tyranny or the senses glut themselves, but the true, wild, pure paradise of the angels. Enter therein, and it will be as if you distilled the essence of 1,000 years of life into a single diamond-radiant drop.

Listen to earthly birdsong, because sensitive, heart-attuned listening, wherein you give your entire being to absorbing the song and actually direct your soul to step right inside it, can transport you to paradise, to the world of the Hyperboreans, for a timeless moment. When the warbler sings to you, paradise opens its arms to you and is all around you. You will recognize it as your birthright.

Waxwing

The waxwing is a bird of fairytale, breeding in dense northern forests where there are old, lichen-covered trees. Its call is a high-pitched, trilling song, like a bell. In colour it is a blush-dun, with shades of grey over its rump. It has a beautifully marked black, yellow and white pattern on its wings, a golden tail-tip, and a stiff row of red spikes at the end of its secondary flight feathers which look as if they were formed from wax. Under its beak and over its eyes it wears a mask of black, because who it truly is remains hidden from human eyes. It wears a crest, for it is a royal bird in its fairy haunts.

Of course, it is also very much present at the earthly level of life. It seeks the tops of trees, because it is a bird of heaven, as we shall see. As well as loving the high places, it will descend onto lower branches, where it sits in perfect stillness and silence, indicating that it is a meditation bird, one that comes to urge us to give the gift of this practice to ourselves. It is tame and friendly to human beings, who can advance very close before it eventually flies away. It is an acrobat, like the tit-mouse family, encouraging us to look at our life-situations from all sorts of unexpected angles.

A story is told of this bird by the Native Americans of the northern United States plains.

> In a beautiful region of forest and prairie, a wicked manito
> or evil spirit had established himself. He had decimated the
> Indian population all around, for he loved to kill and eat
> people. One poor widow had suffered particularly at his
> hands, as she had lost her husband and seven sons to him.
>
> She had one son, the youngest, left to her, and a daughter,
> fair of face and soul, who lived with her in her humble
> lodge near to the dwelling of the manito. Their life was one
> of fear and sorrow, because the manito, who loved best of
> all to eat men and boys, was ever reckoning to see how big
> her son was growing, so that when he attained sufficient
> stature the boy could be captured and eaten.
>
> One day the daughter of the lodge wandered far into the
> woods in search of firewood, and, coming to a fragrant
> bank waving with flowers of every hue, she was delighted
> to lie down on this perfumed couch and rest for a while. As
> she lay half asleep, a bird alighted nearby and sang a song

of such bell-like clarity and beauty that she was entranced. The bird told her that until such time as a maiden would accept him in marriage, he could assume only his bird shape, but that if she would marry him, she would see him in another form.

The girl agreed, and at once the bird became a beautiful, strong-limbed young warrior. They married, and lived together in the widow's lodge, although the widow suspected that he was more than human, as he would sit gazing with love on her daughter, with the light of far-off stars shining from his eyes and casting a strange silvery effulgence over his bride.

He shot a deer with his red-tipped arrows and requested of his wife that when the manito came calling, which they knew he soon would, she should serve him with this meat, into which he had placed a certain enchantment that would remove the manito's power to cheat. Before long, the wicked manito appeared, demanding his right to challenge the newcomer to a race, the winner of which would forfeit his life to the other. This old law was the method the manito used to ensnare men into his power, because, as he was a magician and could change shape during the race into any animal whose speed and force would be useful to him, he always won. The beautiful young husband accepted the manito's challenge, much to the distress of his wife and her family, who were convinced he would die.

On the morning of the great race, the young brave painted his face with tints of red, to show that he was ready for war or peace according to the wish of his challenger. The manito appeared, and the warrior offered to relax the rules of their game, so that no life would become forfeit, on the condition that such a trophy would never be demanded of anyone by the manito again. The manito scornfully refused the offer, and the race began. There then followed an astonishing display of shape-shifting by both competitors in the race, which was difficult even for the magical young brave to win because of the huge strength of the evil power that the manito wielded. But, on seeing his bride waiting for him at the winning-post, the brave made a last valiant effort and won the race, upon which the manito died.

The warrior went on to uproot the black lodge of the manito, and vanquished all his servants. He then led his wife and her family to the fragrant couch of flowers where he had first met his bride, telling them that he must now depart in company with his wife. He explained that the Great Spirit had allowed him to befriend the family to help them in their distress, but that now he had accomplished the task assigned to him, he must return to the heaven worlds. He wished to take his bride with him into the angelic realms, as she was the true companion of his heart.

Both the warrior and his bride thereupon became birds and rose into the air, clothed in shining colours. They disappeared into the ethereal blue, but the widow and her son did not grieve their loss, because they were allowed, whenever they listened, to hear the music of the two birds ever carolling in ecstasy from the heart of paradise. When that music fell from heaven, they knew nothing but joy.

This happy story is the waxwing's signature. It comes to us when we have an important challenge to face, and particularly when we need to call firmly on divine help to see us through. Perhaps this is why a negative interpretation of the bird's augury is the belief that the appearance of an unusually large number of waxwings in any one year foretold war, pestilence, natural disaster and a cruel winter.

The true way to approach the waxwing's auspice is to read the message in its story, and to know that it comes as helpmeet, warrior and rescuer, calling magically to these qualities within ourselves, and to denizens of the spirit world and the angelic realms to come to our aid. It promises a fairytale happy ending after tribulation, and its clear, bell-like tones sing, like music falling from heaven: 'Love is the divine solvent!'

Wheatear

Intriguingly, considering its auspice, this vividly-patterned bird was known in some areas as 'horsematch' because of its habit of flying alongside horse-drawn traps and carriages as if racing them. The pretty wheatear, showing flashes of vivid white as it bobs, runs, and darts in flight over moorland, open lowland pastures and stony heaths, is marked by a pure white tail banded at its tip by a dark T-shape.

This prominent feature concerns its augury, for it is likely to come to you when you arrive at a T-junction in your life! You may be inspired to move forward and be deeply desirous of doing so, but yet, as if you were a chess piece, life will not allow it. No path opens up before you. Instead, you find that you can turn only to the right or to the left. Apart from a retreat, these are the only options open to you. You can stay on the road you are walking only if you retrace your steps.

Draw close to the wheatear in meditation, and consider these options. It might be advisable for you to turn right (a decisive move away from your previously chosen path) or to turn left (a more passive, drifting, 'let's see what might happen now that my way forward has been blocked' outlook) or even to go back. Perhaps there is something along the way that you have missed, and your spiritual guidance is directing you to return for it. However, if you do not wish to retreat or veer off the road you are following, could there be another choice, even though the road ahead is barred?

Although the wheatear is generally a bird of arid, stony, waste places, in tune with the barring and blocking it conveys, this upright, active, restless little bird also loves the sea, and will visit coastal regions, stopping off during migration or even setting up home among grassy sand-dunes near river-mouths as they pour into the sea. Does this bird that loves sandy places and the proximity of water have its own myth, its own fairytale, its own dream? It certainly has.

From the fable-filtered sands of the Arabian Desert it brings lays and minstrelsies composed of tales told in the long-ago of the world.

> One tells of a river, white and pure and born from a hidden and sacred lake, which longed to be taken up into the highest peaks of the mountains but, of course, could not run uphill. Nevertheless, the river resolved to reach the foot of the mountains. Eventually, it came to a stretch of desert sand, and found it could not continue. It threw itself more and more desperately into the sand, determined at all costs to cross the desert, but the situation was hopeless. All that happened was that the sandy path down which the river longed to course gradually began to turn into a swamp.
>
> Eventually, after much tribulation, the river heard a voice, composed of many voices, whispering up from the sand. The voice told the river that it must renounce its violent desperation, change its form into vapour and allow the wind to carry it to the peaks, where it would fall as rain and become a gushing torrent among the mountains, which had always been its heart's desire. Afraid to lose its form, the river hesitated. But it soon realized that in throwing itself across the sands its life was indeed ebbing away; so it ceased its forceful violent battering of itself, and waited in stillness.
>
> The wind blew across the desert, and, listening, the river heard its voice, and recognized within its musical tones the voice of the spirit that it had believed was only upon the mountains. Joyfully, it gave itself up into the arms of the wind, which bore it as vapour high into the distant white peaks. There it fell as rain, and became a rushing mountain torrent, so strong and wild and free that it could bear boulders on its breast and still run its course, liberated forever from barring and blocking and denial of its momentum.

This wonderland story suits the wheatear well, for it nests in rabbit holes! Its call is harsh, although its song is sweet. Country people in times past looked upon it as an omen of wealth or woe, for its emergence as from the netherworlds gave it the status of a prophesying fairy bird. If at first sight of it the bird was on a grassy tuft, or on a low spray of gorse or juniper, the auspice was good. However, if it was initially glimpsed sitting upon a stone or rock, the auspice was bad. Old lore said of the wheatear that it tended to 'haunt old ruins, graveyards and cairns and has gotten a bad name' (recorded in *Where the Forest Murmurs,* by Fiona Macleod).

Yet this little bird, elegant and poised on its long black legs, holds the secret of how to deal creatively with stony ground, death and dissolution in all its forms. Its call is harsh and stony-voiced, uncannily like two stones being knocked together, but its song is mellifluent.

Irrespective of whether it signals good or bad, right or left, the wheatear's counsel is to stop and look, to listen deep within, and then, perhaps, to catch the voice of the wind of the spirit, and offer yourself up to it without resistance. Let it carry you. This is how to overcome the riddle of the T-junction!

The wheatear sweetly warbles, with the Sufi master who first told the story of the river and its dream, 'The river of life is an eternal path, and its destiny is written in the sands.'

Whimbrel

Old lore tells of the whimbrel, whose Gaelic name is flute-note or mellow-whistle, that it neither eats nor drinks but feeds upon the wind, and all its hunting quests after the pathless regions of the air. Fiona Macleod says of this bird: 'The Cornish or Devon moorlander has many wild tales of the whimbrel, whose swift-repeated whistle hurtling suddenly in lonely places has given rise to innumerable legends.'

This 'little curlew' is a bird that celebrates the imagination. When it comes to you, it may bring a warning as one of the renowned Seven Whistlers, for, like all such birds, its haunting, lonely whistle sounds in bursts of seven; but it is much more likely to seek to stimulate and release the force of your imagination with its wheeling flight and evocative cries. This great God-given power is almighty.

The whimbrel sings with wild and heart-piercing music: 'You were created in the Imagination of God – and God has given you the ultimate and incalculable gift of Imagination!'

Whinchat (*see also* STONECHAT)

The augury of the whinchat is similar to that of the stonechat, except that in the case of the whinchat it pinpoints the sense of seeing rather than hearing. Nurture your eyesight; close your eyes, turn them to the Sun, massage your shut eyelids gently with your fingertips in a clockwise circle, turn your eyes away from the Sun, and open them again. When you care for your eyes often in this way, and glance from their corners, you will begin to see the fairies, for this little bird of forest, moor and meadow is a fairy bird.

The whinchat cries, with gentle scolding mockery: 'You say "Seeing is believing"; I say, "Believing is seeing"!'

Whitethroat (including **Lesser Whitethroat**)

With its subtly peaked crown and its long tail, the little whitethroat flits from hedge to hedge, reluctant to allow itself to be seen. In its spiritual essence, the whitethroat is a bird in waiting. It is symbolic of self-abnegation. Its song is unmusical and it keeps under cover. Its throat-feathers, as its name declares, are pure white.

It comes to us when we, too, are in waiting, when we are being prepared, as it were, for the next level of life. This may be a time when your light is obscured, your qualities unseen, the dynamics of your personality ignored, and your gifts unnoticed. The whitethroat counsels you to wait in tranquillity, because an important centre, the throat chakra, is undergoing a process of purification and quickening, and it is important that you remain under cover as a personality so that you are left in peace whilst this process completes itself.

For a time it will be as if you moved within the swathes of a white veil, so that those around you see you as if through a mist. This is a protective shield, because it is as if you have re-entered the womb. Your spiritual evolutionary dynamic is adding to and perfecting a part of your soul-temple. You are in the workshop.

The throat chakra is our communication centre, our inner listening centre; when you emerge from the workshop, your deeper being will be tuned to a new scale, higher and more advanced than before. Your song will come into its own. For now, the whitethroat from the depths of its bush asks you to be at peace, and let things ride.

The story of the whitethroat is called 'The Singing Apple' (the apple signifies the fruition of a higher order of knowledge or wisdom – a perceptuality – coming into being within the soul).

> The singing apple was an enchanted apple crafted
> from a single huge ruby on a stem of golden amber.
> It had the power to inspire anyone to anything by the
> breath of its fragrance, and enabled the one into whose care
> it was given to write verses of the highest eloquence and to
> compose music or speak words that made listeners laugh
> with joy or weep with poignant sorrow. The enchanted
> apple itself sang so as to ravish the ear with an
> unimaginable beauty of sound.
>
> It was guarded by a dragon with three heads, which had
> kept it so long that the rumour of it had become fable. A
> prince who was determined to win it put on armour of
> glass, which constituted a thousand mirrors, and advanced
> on the unconquerable dragon. The dragon, on seeing its
> reflection a thousand times in the armour-mirrors, thought
> that a great concourse of rival dragons was marching on it,
> and ran into its cave.
>
> The prince, having retrieved the singing apple, left the
> dragon's lair and blocked up the entrance so that it could
> not follow him.

To un-riddle this tale, we see that the singing apple is the new state of awareness that is being forged within the soul that the whitethroat symbolizes, the dragon is the old self or the ego which will not allow the singing apple to work its wonders or to pass out of its lair, and the prince is the new self waiting to claim the treasure. The new self does this by biding its time and, through applying the law of reflection, by compelling the ego to retreat in confusion. It then seizes the singing apple and bears it away in triumph, having disempowered the blockings and denials of the old self. As we see, the singing apple has to dwell in the dragon's cave for a time, and the ego has to be quelled, before this wondrous treasure can be won by the prince.

Therefore, have no fear because life forbids you to shine for the moment. The whitethroat cries: 'Patience is the sea of peace from which your life will rise newly-born and radiant!'

Wigeon (see also DUCK)

The augury brought by the wigeon is similar to that of the duck, except that the wigeon, with its roseate breast, golden forehead and pearly underparts, asks you to purify your emotions so that you may receive nothing less than enlightenment. The wigeon bears both a challenging and a golden auspice. You are about to receive a crown. The wigeon counsels you to wear it well.

Woodcock (see also SNIPE and JACK SNIPE)

The woodcock brings the same augury as the snipe and the jack snipe, except that this bird is particularly associated with Merlin, and with Oberon, king of the fairies. If you were king of the fairies, or prince of enchanters, what would you do? How would you use your power? Merlin is the wise sage whose circumspection balances the youthful dynamic of Oberon.

If you can find a colour picture or photograph of a woodcock, use it as a focus for meditation, and lose yourself in the mystical, shamanic patterning of its plumage. There are eyes and worlds, flames and rivers, dancing shadow puppets with a message, to be found therein.

The woodcock, elf-like, builds its nest in a hollow near a tree or in a bower in the undergrowth. If its young are threatened, the intrepid and resourceful woodcock expresses its protective virtues by carrying the nestlings one by one between its legs to a place of safety.

The collective noun for this bird is a fall, and a fall of woodcocks was believed to arrive overnight on the back of an easterly wind at the end of October, on Samhain evening or Hallowe'en. This swelling of the resident population by flocks of winter migrants was heralded as almost a spirit visitation. It was looked for eagerly, and if the woodcocks arrived early, a bountiful 'harvest home' was expected for the following year. If the last of the hay had not yet been gathered in, however, the omen was ominous and ruin almost inevitable.

These winter-visiting woodcocks were supposed to enshrine a magical essence even over and above that of the resident flock. It was believed that they flew to the Moon for the summer, spending it in strange shining days and nights upon the pearly lunar plains. The effect of the moon-summer was alchemical and mysterious, granting the woodcock many powers. The seasonal return to the Moon was understood as a return to the womb of the Virgin in oirder to be initiated as an enchanter.

The sacred masculine principle dwelling in both genders is the focus of the woodcock's auspice. It is time to express this masculinity in a new way, free from the constraints and the stranglehold of the mundane, conventional stereotypes and cultural prejudices that often hold sway. You can be as a man touched with magic; and if this auspice comes to a woman, it speaks either to the yang balance within her, or to a man or a boy connected with her. It is time for this man, whether dwelling within a woman or without her, to find his magical, miracle-working self, which is sourced in the heart of the Great Mother, and to strike the balance between wise Merlin and impulsive Oberon.

Finding the balance is important, because the woodcock was once famous for walking straight into traps! To avoid the myriad snares set on the path of one who responds to the call of the magical self, the youthful Oberon must venerate Merlin the sage. When you balance the aspects within you in this way, you will find yourself operating within the unutterably bright imagination of God, and your soul will rejoice in its freedom.

Woodlark (see SKYLARK)

Woodpecker (All Types)

The handsome green woodpecker is a bird of prophecy, and as a rain bird, bringing soft vernal showers to succour the earth, it is a bird of motherhood and compassion.

In ancient Roman legend, Picus, sometimes cited as the first king in Italy, was the son of Saturn, and a renowned soothsayer who drew his wisdom from a close study of the Language of the Birds. He was helped in his auguries by a green woodpecker, his totem bird. He was depicted in art as a young man with a woodpecker perching on his head, so linking the bird with his seat of consciousness. Picus fell in love with the tree-goddess Pomona (some representations of Picus show him as a tree or a pillar of wood) but he was loved by the sorceress Circe; and when he repulsed her advances she transmogrified him into a woodpecker. As he retained his prophetic powers in his bird shape, the green woodpecker became a bird of prophecy.

It is also the bird that aided the she-wolf in feeding and rearing Romulus and Remus, the founders of Rome, who were the twin sons of Silvia and Mars. As Silvia is the goddess of trees and woodland, her motherly spirit expressed itself through the maternal woodpecker by co-nurturing her children. A Roman coin supposedly exists which is engraved with two woodpeckers sitting in a sacred fig-tree whilst a wolf feeds twin boys beneath its branches.

Trees, especially the fig tree, are emblems of the Goddess, and when the woodpecker comes to you, Divine Mother holds you in her embrace of love and wisdom, and gently soothes and nurtures your soul, bringing healing balm for your wounds, whether sustained from life's stony path, or from the process of growth and putting forth.

Woodpigeon (see DOVE and PIGEON)

Wren

Always a delight to spot scurrying about between bushes like a busy mouse, the tiny wren, so delicate in appearance, is one of Britain's most resilient birds, outfacing even the harshest winters.

This bird, representing humility, was the sacred bird of sacrifice for the New Year. The Earth Goddess was said to select her truest son, a God-king, for her annual sacrificial rites, who would willingly undertake the role to pay the debts of the passing year to propitiate the dark earth powers, and to usher in the new dispensation of light and life. Although it is said by the great mystagogues of the past and the present that the use of blood-sacrifice in such ceremonies is a crude physical interpretation, an insufficiently transcendental understanding of a deep and beautiful spiritual truth (which is that we must willingly sacrifice our own lower selves to receive the incoming tide of the spirit and not other people or animals!), this does not lessen the mystical significance of the wren.

In many parts of northern Europe, the wren was called 'the King', and was killed at Christmas or on Twelfth Night (Christmas Day in the old calendar). A Christianized variation of the old pagan rites was to kill it on St Stephen's Day (26 December), as it supposedly alerted the guards when St Stephen tried to escape from imprisonment, thereby assuring the death of the first English martyr.

That it was a protected bird, a 'bird of honour', which it was considered taboo to hunt or harm at any other time of the year gives the lie to the Christian tradition. The bird is beloved of the Goddess (in many country districts it was called 'Our Lady's Hen') and was considered not only a bird of prophecy by the Druids, but was also held in greatest reverence. To the ancient Irish the wren was a bird of powerful sorcery and was called 'the Druid Bird'. The Welsh word *Dryw* means both 'Druid' and 'wren'. The Scots held it to be a bird of blessing, and in an old Scottish rhyme which curses those who would harm the wren, it is again connected with the Goddess (in the guise of Mary):

> Malaisons, malaisons mair that ten
> That harry our Lady of Heaven's wren.

The wren's kingship seems to be linked with the oak, the sacred tree of the Father-God in Druidism. The wren's nest was known as 'the Druid's House'. The reason that the powerful and respected Druid was referred to as a little wren can be discovered in the telling of an old tale from Scotland.

> All the birds of the air assembled in a great company to decide who should be their king. It was agreed that the bird who flew highest of all should be given the title. The bird to triumph in this contest was the eagle, who claimed his entitlement to kingship in resounding voice as he rose far above all others.
>
> Just as he did so, the little wren shot out from under the eagle's feathers where he had been hiding, and, fluttering upwards a little higher than his unwitting carrier, cried, 'Birds of the air, look up and behold your king!'

This is a story of the supremacy of mind, or consciousness, over the power of the physical body, and it truly represented the Druid, whose powers of spirit, psyche, and learning were considered superior to those of simple physicality. This recognition of 'mind over matter' or the 'kingship' of the soul and spirit over the body was a new dispensation in the Age of Aries to which the Druids belonged. The Age of Aries was the age of 'sheep' or common humanity being led forward in its evolution by 'shepherds', wise kings or masters who had humanity in their keeping, as demonstrated by the 'shepherds' and the Three Wise Kings, the upholders of the old regime who came to visit Christ, the king of the new era of Pisces.

The wren, then, was the magical bird-symbol of this new Age of Aries, of Wise Ones; and the little humble brown bird, the Druid bird, looked forward down the bright star-trails of time not only to the Age of Pisces, the age of Christ the Fisher King (there is an old Celtic legend which says that the wren was once a mermaid, linking it with the watery Piscean era), but to the new Age of Aquarius, when the mind would be subsumed into the powers of the spirit, and the Christ-forces, which the Druids understood and recognized, would be released in humanity and sail above the gravity pull of the Earth as the White One, the great bird of peace and freedom, symbolized by the albatross and the white eagle. And yet the wren was protected by the old era, the ancient energies of the Taurean Age.

Prior to the Age of Aries was the Taurean Age, the great era of physical struggle and valour, represented by the bull-muscled hero of the age, Hercules or Heracles, who through his twelve great labours created the twelve sacred channels (one for each sign of the zodiac) for the spiritual powers to be called down to our planet through the stars and to be earthed via humanity itself. It is said that Hercules incarnated as a God-man and walked the Earth in a physical body. Physicality was the medium of spiritual manifestation and needed to be exalted in those far-off days; but this gave rise to some forms of belief, behaviour and worship which denied the spirit, and which created an obscurity or confusion which had to be lifted.

Legend tells us that the wren on its nest, hatching the eggs of the new dispensation, is guarded by the bull-god Taranis (a Celtic form of Taurus) who strikes via thunder and lightning if anyone is foolish enough to try to steal the wren's precious eggs – just as we, in this new age of Aquarius, will be protected by the energies of the old era, symbolized by the wren, who brings to us lessons of humility, of the precedence of the spirit over earthly claims, and of the eternal wisdom, to keep us safe on our road into the heart of the breaking dawn.

Spiritual teachers, and the angels themselves, tell us that when birds die, their spirits, so closely linked with the angels, pass into the heart of nature; that 'nature within nature', the dynamic paradise out of which all manifesting natural forms arise and are born onto the Earth. There, their joyous spirits merge with the Hidden People, the folk of the secret fairy races who ensoul and make manifest the nature kingdom, to help and inspire them in their cosmic task; and from there, the bird-spirits sometimes evolve, through unimagined aeons of time, into great angelic beings whose ministrations involve planets other than Earth.

Is it not said by those who see angels that their wings manifest sometimes as arcs of shining light, and sometimes actually as feathered pinions? These latter, it would seem, still hold close to their hearts the energy-patterns of their original bird-forms. And why should this not be so, when birds and angels exist in such spiritual harmony?

Esoteric teaching tells us that the Earth is older than we can imagine, and that these mysteries of origin have not yet been fully revealed to us. Until they are, we can only be sure that the angels keep their ancient places, and that the spiritual reality of birds existed long before this planet came into being.

When the wren comes to you, it comes as a vivid symbol of life. It brings good tidings, and alerts you to an approaching situation that will initiate a new cycle in your life. The wren is both your initiator and protector, teaching you to call on reserves of resilience and integrity secreted in your deepest being which may never have been challenged before. You may need to proceed with care and humility, with discernment and intelligence both intuitive and analytical. Your acts of innovation and valiance may need to keep a low profile, or even be hidden at first. Remember that this bird is an invoker of powerful forces, and reassures you that the secret, magical tides of the universe – 'the force' – will work with you as you bravely take each new step into the unknown. There may be a sacrificial requirement, but this sacrifice will release a dynamic surge of light into your consciousness and onto your life path. If you are careful to sacrifice an aspect of yourself rather than principles or other people, you will take your place among the true, realized, children of Earth, beloved of the Goddess and wrapped around in her mantle of initiating power, protection and blessings.

Wryneck

The wryneck is an enigmatic bird. It has links with the nightjar, and therefore the hawk family, although it is also a relative of the woodpecker. It is hardly larger than a house sparrow, and yet it behaves like a thrush, a species of the enchanting company of the Birds of Beautiful Song (*see* pages 5–9). Like a bunting, it spends much of its time on the ground. It has the royal crest (*see* PHEASANT), although, being a shy and somehow humble little bird, its crest is small and seldom raised. Its plumage is dun and sombre, yet is impressively marked with brown beads and bars and arrowheads and the cascading patterns of the Otherworld.

Most intriguing of all, it gains its name from the fact that when it is alarmed, it raises its understated crest, spreads its tail and twists its neck vigorously from side to side like a snake.

It is falcon-bird with the snake in its talons (*see* EAGLE); it is reminiscent of the bird of beautiful song; it is a bird of the day, yet it is linked with the night-hawk (*see* NIGHTJAR); it is royal, yet humble and retiring; it speaks of little things, like the bunting, and yet its cousin is Picus, great Lord of Augury, illustrious keeper of bird-wisdom.

The wryneck is nothing if not a conundrum, and when it comes to you, it approaches to show you that, beneath a humble and unremarkable exterior, the path to your dreams will be laid before you. It will not shine with lustre, but its hidden light is as the radiance of diamonds in their shadowed underground chambers. Once the Sun begins to shine, your world will be filled with measureless light. Reconciling opposites, this bird unfailingly hits the mark. It carries the secret of the serpent, which is the secret of radiating light from within.

It bids you contemplate the concept of hidden treasure enclosed within a battered casket; and its stirring, falcon-like, far-carrying cry articulates, like music on the wind: 'All things are possible!'

Yellowhammer

This delightful yellow bunting (called 'hammer' after *ammer*, German for 'bunting') was once a fairly common sight, although its numbers have declined by more than half since 1970. Much sinister folklore attaches itself to this friendly, innocuous little bird. One typical story cites that it fluttered round Christ as he died on the Cross, and the drops of blood it disturbed with its restless flight transferred themselves forever afterwards to its eggs.

However, it seems likely that the bird was revered by the Druids, and that it was known as 'the little bird of Mercury'. The bird of Mercury was the messenger bird between the shaman and the gods. It also sought out knowledge from the underworld and from across the globe for the questing adept, and brought back this wisdom to its human associate. Its colour, which links with Mercury, was a bright, brilliant yellow, representing the colour of the sanctified mind radiant with the light of the spirit.

Because of its connection with the Druid priests, and because they themselves also associated the yellowhammer with the Sun deity and with Brigid, Goddess of the Morning Star (sometimes Mercury, sometimes Venus), later bigotry associated the bird with Lucifer. It was supposed to receive a drop of the devil's blood every May Day morning. (Some superstitions cited every May and every Monday or moon-day morning for the dispensation of this diabolical blood; May and Monday are the month and the day sacred to the Goddess.) The devil's blood was supposed to be signified by the red-brown speckles on its breast.

These speckles, in addition to the satanic designation, led to the belief that a toad hatched the eggs of the yellowhammer, although this seems rooted in gleams of the half-forgotten awareness that the knowledge of the Serpent People (*see* IBIS) and the knowledge of the Druids, albeit diminished in the latter case, were one. The yellowhammer eggs that the toad hatched in the nest were believed to include a number of snake hatchlings. The reputation of the Toad-Stone, a golden stone secreted in the heads of toads which gave its possessor access to cosmic and timeless wisdom, was of the highest among the Druids, and the animal was esteemed as holy by them.

In Wales, the seat of Druidism, the yellowhammer was called *gwas y neidr*, 'servant of the snake', because of its messenger status between the druidic priesthood and the gods, and because it was so in harmony with the sacred serpent that it warned snakes of approaching danger.

To the interpretive ear the yellowhammer's song has a strange affinity with human speech, and many have heard within its vocal configurations the likeness of the words: Whetil te, whetil te, whee! Harry my nest and the de'il take ye!; 'little-bit-of-bread-and-no-cheese'; and 'pretty-pretty-creature'.

The markings on the yellowhammer's eggs can be seen to resemble scribbled writings like cabbalistic signs. Because of this, it was known as the 'writing-lark', the 'writing-master' or the 'scribe'. An anonymous verse describes these writings:

> Five eggs, pen scribbled o'er with ink their shells
> Resembling writing-scrolls, which Fancy reads
> As nature's poesy and pastoral spells –
> They are the yellowhammer's.

When the yellowhammer comes to you, you are indeed being visited by 'the little bird of Mercury'. It is the bird of messages, the bird of wisdom, and it is the writer's bird, encompassing all writing categories, especially those that lean to the mystical and creative. It will bring back knowledge, spiritual gold, from the higher worlds. It will bridge any disconnection between you and your deepest spirit.

It particularly comes to people who are rejected or ridiculed or persecuted for their talents or the calibre of their message, who have something to convey to the world that the world would rather overlook. These are the 'children of the dark star', the star that seems to bring trepidation and suffering, but in essence is truly radiant, brilliantly golden as the yellowhammer's bright plumage.

This little bird brings hope, cheer, comfort, the inspiration to keep on keeping on. It bids you take up the tools of your endeavour and wield them afresh, though they may seem like a burden and a torment, for your day will dawn. The yellowhammer's rich, jubilant song ever repeats: 'Stay centred always in the heart of the light blazing from the spiritual spheres, and you will come through!'

The Story of The Hawk of Achill: Its Links with the Emerald Tablet and the Holy Grail

*I*f we retreat in time to about 6,000 years ago, the approximate age of the salmon in the story of *The Hawk of Achill*, we find evidence on clay tablets inscribed by the ancient Sumerians that the renowned Emerald Tablet was held at that time by the guardians of their civilization. It was given to the world as an act of divine grace after a terrible blow befell the Earth and the peoples of the Earth, as shall be disclosed. The Emerald Tablet, a natural artefact containing sacred technology, was patterned with what might be imagined as light-energy ideographs held deep within the stone, which encoded all the knowledge that could ever be given to planet Earth and her peoples.

The guardians of the Sumerian civilization were the 'gods', superhumans who had high-vibrational bodies composed of non-physical atoms and who had come, according to the clay tablets, from another planet in our solar system to initiate the development of human life on Earth. There were two royal brothers among these 'gods'. The birthright of one was to assume kingship over his own people and over developing humanity on Earth (ourselves).

This brother, Enki, followed the injunctions of Divine Spirit, doing all he could, together with his consort, to civilize physical humankind evolving in simian bodies and to lead them by the God-light within themselves to the same level of cosmic evolution as that which the gods enjoyed. He loved humanity and served it faithfully; the light of God blazed forth from his heart, and he was known on Earth as the John-man, or Oannes, the man who came from the sea.

The other brother, Enlil, despised humanity, was disgusted by its physicality and brutishness which he thought degraded the blood of the superhuman race to which he belonged and which had initiated earthly humans with its own DNA, and longed for nothing more than a planetary ethnic cleansing. He decided that any God who would wish to implant divine humanity (for the 'gods', although superhuman by our standards, were nevertheless human) into animal bodies functioning at the slow, heavy, physical level of life (its outermost limits) must actually be demonic and not God at all. He began to suspect that in fact he himself was God, or that God was a sort of reflection of his own ego, operating from the highest heavens. He further decided that it was his personal mission and duty to permanently obliterate all human life on Earth and to seal off disgusting matter, this obscene 'outermost limit' of manifestation, from penetration by the 'gods' for all time, simply for their own good.

Not realizing that these urges arose in him because he himself had become unbalanced in his consciousness, in his humanity and in his connection with his own greater self or spirit due to the mighty challenge of the material forces working on Earth, he usurped the kingship and entered into continuing battle with Enki, ever seeking, by ingenious means, to lead humanity to its own destruction. (He could not simply kill it outright because of universal law, although he made a concerted attempt on more than one occasion.)

His most heinous act was to cut off the planetary connection between God and the Earth, to which every human being was intimately linked and which gave them fully conscious access to the higher worlds of the spirit. This beautiful connection to God, which was like a magical ladder between heaven and Earth (in fact it looked like a spiral stairway, or a serpent of light), was called the Grail, 'such a holy thing', as Tennyson, writing thousands of years later with inspired vision, described it. Humanity's only fully conscious connection to God after the destruction of the Grail (it could never be entirely destroyed) remained deeply secreted within the heart.

The Emerald Tablet, from which the Green Language, or the Language of the Birds, was transcribed, was given to the Earth at this time to help humanity to begin the process of ascension once more, but Enlil found a way to withhold it. Now deaf and blind to the fulsome reality of the spirit and the higher worlds, human beings could only experience God by moving towards this little flickering light shining within the darkness of their own vision. Many declined to do so, which cast civilization after civilization onto a path of self-destruction, aided and abetted and invisibly influenced by the connivances of Enlil, who worked through the mind and the intellect of humanity as well as its lower urges, which he delighted in inflating.

Enlil's second heinous act was to hide the Emerald Tablet in a secret dimension which could never be penetrated. He then released a false Emerald Tablet out into the world, containing only partial truths derived from the original, indiscernibly and invidiously blended with horrific death forces whose influences have kept humankind locked in a deadly reverse-spin ever since.

How does this story, partly outlined on ancient clay tablets, connect with the merlin and The Hawk of Achill? The Druids were connected with a global brotherhood that followed the teachings of Enki (later called Masda or Thoth, whose famous pupil was Hermes or Zoroaster), Enki took on the name of Oannes (Johannes or the John-man of the Mandeans) and served in the Temple of Oannes, which was dedicated to the Father God (the Fish-man). The enormous difference between this Father God and the Enlil-inspired way we view Father God today is that the symbol of Oannes was a fish, showing us that Father God taught that he was a fish or a serpent, or to be precise, a spermatozoa swimming in the waters of the Great Mother.

In other words, Father God was an aspect of Mother God, brought forth from her depths in an act of unconscionable love so that creation could come into being. This does not detract from the perfect equality between the Father aspect of God and the Mother aspect, but it does place him in his true context – sourced in the heart of the Mother and manifested by the Mother, rather than some supreme being who created the feminine principle as an afterthought, in order that she might pleasure and serve the masculine principle.

It was this great truth concerning the Father that Enlil simply could not handle, as his unbalanced psyche saw in it the threat that perhaps the female, the symbol of the Source and the All, was superior to the male, which of course is as nonsensical as the opposite view. Unable to perceive this, Enlil conceived a reactionary hatred and scorn for the feminine principle, and set about denying and demeaning it in every way possible.

Enki's followers, (the Druids, the Essenes, and many earlier and later brotherhoods who were party to a greater or lesser degree to his secret) heroically resisted these influences, although they were so insidious and so cunningly applied that it was difficult to do so entirely. In the story of *The Hawk of Achill*, the salmon might be seen as Enki, or Oannes the Fish-man, enshrining the secret of the Father and the knowledge of the Holy Grail in his sacred pool or source within the Mother.

When Enlil cut away the Grail, a terrible cold fell over the Earth (which appears actually to have happened, if ancient stories of the ancestors of many tribal peoples around the world are accurate accounts), and Enki's eyes were plucked out (his vision was taken) by the hawk of Achill. The hawk took the Fish-man's vision to safeguard it for humankind, because after the great (ethical) freeze, it could no longer be accessed because humanity had been disconnected from it. It had become a blind eye. The hawk of Achill is the merlin, and Merlin (the wiseman, allied to nature, whose knowledge lives on imperceptibly in the secret recesses of the psyche of humankind) keeps for us Enki's vision, or the principle of ascension which the merlin itself embodies – the Grail – the 'Achilles' Heel' of the ingenious, god-like ones who seek to destroy humanity. It is promised that the Grail will return. Another terrible 'night of cold' will fall on the peoples of the Earth (is it even now approaching?), and the merlin, the smallest, most magical of the hawk family, associated with the feminine principle because it is the 'lady's' hawk, will fly to the nest of the eagle, the greatest of the birds of prey, and supplant her offspring. He himself, bearing Enki's vision and Enki's secrets, ready to be given again to misled humankind, will become the new and true reigning eagle – the Eagle of God-knowledge. This means that what the sacred eagle has, through Enlil's canny influence, degenerated into – a symbol of military might and the power of the prince of this world, the power of darkness – will be cast aside and reborn again as the merlin, which will then transform into the true eagle of St John – the phoenix. The deepest, most ancient knowledge will prevail, and truth will shed her healing sunlight over the suffering and the darkness and the terrible cold of the world. This is demonstrated by the merlin's second act. After he supplants the eagle fledgling, he sends the eagle out on a wisdom-quest in which the truth of Enki will gradually be restored to her initially resistant consciousness.

The female eagle in the story is important as a symbol of that ignorance which nurtures and perpetuates the cycle of oppression; and, of course, when the male psyche sees itself bathed in a new light and throws off the chains of Enlil, the veiled and denied female psyche will also be healed and renewed. Traditionally, it has always been understood that the Grail is a purely feminine energy – in fact, according to the secret of Oannes, the very essence of God.

An Esoteric Interpretation
of the Story of the Yellow Dwarf

*I*t is Fair-Star's mission to go to the fount of wisdom, or the oasis in the desert, guided by her mother, and it is the king's mission to make Fair-Star his bride. In this way, they will fulfil their sacred quest of conjoinment and seamless union, and will become guardians and conveyors of the Bright Knowledge. But something goes awry. The Yellow Dwarf enchants the queen and her daughter, and tricks them into thinking that he holds the power of life and death over them. The Yellow Dwarf is a distorted and truncated form of the Golden or Bright Knowledge, meaning that Fair-Star has somehow allowed herself to be influenced in her understanding of it by receiving it from others in the form of cant and dogma, rather than trusting to the pristine and incorruptible fountain of wisdom within her heart. It has become dwarfed, debased, and treacherous. She has to flee from the illusory lions down stairs of brass or base metal, and sets sail on an 'underground stream' (a well-known esoteric allusion) which, had it been the true one, would have manifested as bright rather than tarnished silver. This false underground stream lulls her to sleep again, and when she and her mother awaken, they find themselves back in their palace, as though they had never set out to seek wisdom – only now, unsurprisingly, they are sick. Fair-Star's wedding day is doomed, because she cannot find the Pole Star or conjoin herself with the Golden Mountain. The Yellow Dwarf is bound to carry her off and imprison her, which he does. The king, likewise, becomes imprisoned by the fount of knowledge (the desert spirit) which would have activated and initiated the living waters in his bride, unable to draw from it but equally unable to tear himself away, even though it leaves him parched and wandering. At last he finds the midnight sea, and an archetypal symbol of the sacred feminine wisdom, the mermaid, comes to his rescue. She puts into his hands the implement which will rescue both the lovers and deliver them to the union of the wedding-chamber. The king slays all the creatures which stand between himself and his beloved bride – but he has forgotten, or not properly comprehended, the power of the Yellow Dwarf. He cannot see that the 34 creatures separating him from her, which reduce to a numerological resolution of seven – the seven stages of the soul – are only mirror-images of the dwarf. He does not realize that he must free Fair-Star from the dwarf's tyranny and restore her to herself. He needed to do this by cutting away what ultimately stood between them – the Yellow Dwarf himself. And it has been the Yellow Dwarf who has been claiming Fair-Star's hand in marriage all along; in other words, the false, crude, indoctrinating, outer-sourced knowledge has embattled the true understanding of it from the start. He virtually hands over the diamond sword, whose virtue is to make all illusion transparent. As soon as the sword falls into the hands of the Yellow Dwarf, its power reverses and becomes a hideous mockery of itself. The king and his rightful bride are now entirely in the power of the Yellow Dwarf; and when he will not renounce her and thereby acknowledge his powerlessness, the antago- nized dwarf strikes the king dead with the diamond sword, at which point Fair-Star herself expires in grief. Now, in death, the two lovers are one, and free at last from the evil dwarf and his castle Steel-Heart (its name indicating the result of receiving the Bright Knowledge in a partial, distorted and manipulated way). But their quest is essentially lost, because their union should have taken place on Earth, and joined the Pole Star and the Golden Mountain in glorious union within human con- sciousness itself. Too late, the king realizes with his expiring breath that the Yellow Dwarf is a deviant, dangerous and chaotic part of his own psyche, which was why it was able to seize the sword that belonged to him and pervert its power. It was his duty to transform the dwarf by slaying the creature with the sword that cuts through illusion, and free himself and his bride forever. Now he has put his own power into its hands, the unharmonized part of his psyche takes its dreadful and insane revenge by slaying him and Fair-Star. They both fall on the sword that was designed to save them, whilst Fair-Star's mother returns sadly to source, unable to participate in the life of the world any longer.

Brigid of the Isles

S peaking of the many Gaelic names of beauty and reverence for Brigid, Fiona Macleod says: They refer to one who in the dim far-off days of the forgotten pagan world of our ancestors was a noble and great goddess. They refer to one to whom the women of the Gael went with offerings and prayers, as went the women of ancient Hellas to the temple of Aphrodite, as went the Syrian women to the altars of Astarte, as went the women of Egypt to the milk-fed shrines of Isis. They refer to one whom the Druids held in honour as a torch bearer of the eternal light, a Daughter of the Morning, who held sunrise in one hand as a little yellow flame, and in the other held the red flower of fire without which men would be as the beasts who live in caves and holes, or as the dark *Fomor* who have their habitations in cloud and wind and the wilderness. They refer to one whom the bards and singers revered as mistress of their craft, she whose breath was a flame, and that flame song: she whose secret name was fire and whose inmost soul was radiant air, she therefore who was the divine impersonation of the divine thing she stood for, Poetry.

> 'St. Bride of the Kindly Fire'... is she, that ancient goddess, whom our ancestors saw lighting the torches of sunrise on the brows of hills, or thrusting the quenchless flame above the horizons of the sea: whom the Druids hailed with hymns at the turn of the year, when, in the season we call February, the firstcomers of the advancing Spring are to be

seen on the grey land or on the grey wave or by the grey
shores: whom every poet, from the humblest wandering
singer to Oisin of the Songs, from Oisin of the songs to
Angus Og on the rainbow or to Midir of the Underworld,
blessed, because of the flame she put in the heart of poets
as well as the red life she put in the flame that springs from
wood and peat...Was she not born at sunrise? On the day
she reached womanhood did not the house wherein she
dwelled become wrapped in a flame which consumed it
not, though the crown of that flame licked the high
unburning roof of Heaven?

In that hour when, her ancient divinity relinquished and
she reborn a Christian saint, she took the white veil, did
not a column of golden light rise from her head till no eyes
could follow it? In that moment when she died from Earth,
having taken mortality upon her so as to know a divine
resurrection to a new and still more enduring Country of
the Immortal, were there not wings of fire seen flashing
along all the shores of the west and upon the summits of all
Gaelic hills? And how could one forget that at any time she
had but to bend above the dead, and the breath would
quicken, and a pulse would come back into the still heart,
and what was dust would arise and be once more glad.

Here is her special benediction, The Blessing of Brigid, which can be
intoned if you feel afraid or vulnerable.

The Blessing Of Brigid

Brigid of the mantles,
Brigid of the bright flame,
Brigid of the twining hair,
Brigid of the augury.

Brigid of the white feet,
Brigid of serenity,
Brigid of the white palms,
Brigid of the kine.

Brigid, companion-woman,
Brigid of the heart's true flame,
Brigid, aid to women,
Brigid, woman kindly.

Brigid, own tress of Mary,
Brigid, nurse of Christ,
Each day and each night
That I intone the blessing of Brigid,

I shall not be slain,
I shall not be wounded,
I shall not be prisoned,
I shall not be gashed,
I shall not be torn in sunder,
I shall not be plundered,
I shall not be down-trodden,
I shall not be stripped,
I shall not be rent in two,
In mind, in body, in soul, in spirit,
Nor shall the Son of Peace let me be forgotten.

Nor sun shall burn me,
Nor fire shall burn me,

Nor beam shall burn me,
Nor moon shall burn me.

Nor river shall drown me,
Nor salt-water drown me,
Nor flood drown me,
Nor water drown me.
In mind, in body, in soul, in spirit.

Nightmare shall not lie on me,
Black-sleep shall not lie on me,
Spell-sleep shall not lie on me,
Sleep-sickness shall not lie on me,
In mind, in body, in soul, in spirit.

I am under the keeping
Of the great Mother of All,
My companion dear to me
Is Brigid.

The beautiful Celtic blessing, which also has potent protective powers, is associated with Brigid. Some sources say that Brigid imparted this blessing to humanity. A shortened version is given below.

Deep peace of the running wave to you,
Deep peace of the flowing air to you,
Deep peace of the quiet earth to you,
Deep peace of the shining stars to you,
Deep peace of the Son of Peace to you,
Smiling calm of Brigid the White to you...

In her childhood, Fiona Macleod, who died in the early years of the 20th century, had a supernatural encounter on one of the Western Isles with Brigid. It remained with her all her life and profoundly influenced her work as a writer, poet, dramatist and spiritual philosopher. She encountered Brigid again in her womanhood, when an old woman she was visiting had a vivid and beautifully evocative dream about her. In the dream, Brigid promised, like King Arthur and the Holy Grail, that she would return again to the world, bringing blessing, healing and the fire of the spirit in her open hands as gifts of the new age.

INDEX

albatross 18
auk, little 18–19
avocet 19

bank swallow *see* house martin
barnacle goose 20 *see also* goose
bar-tailed godwit 55
bean goose 58 *see also* goose
bearded tit 171
bee-eater 20–1
bittern 21 *see also* heron
blackbird 21–2, 86, 87, 90–1
blackcap 22–3
black grouse 64–5 *see also*
    capercaillie
black guillemot 66
black-necked grebe 62
black redstart 128 *see also*
    redstart
black-tailed godwit 55
black-throated diver 37
black-throated loon *see* black-
    throated diver
black-winged stilt 160
blue tit 14, 25
bluebird 23–4
bluethroat 24–5
brambling 26 *see also* chaffinch;
    finch
brent goose 58 *see also* goose
bullfinch 48 *see also* finch
bunting 26 *see also* finch
buzzard 26

Canada goose 58 *see also* goose
capercaillie 27–8
chaffinch 28, 48 *see also* finch
chiffchaff 28
chough 29
coal tit 171
cock 29–31
common loon *see* great northern
    diver
common murre *see* guillemot
common partridge 102 *see also*
    partridge
common redpoll 48 *see also* finch
common scoter 142 *see also* duck
coot 31
cormorant 31–2
corncrake 32
crake, spotted 32–3
crane *see* heron
crested tit 171
crossbill 49
    Scottish 51
    see also finch
crow 33 *see also* raven
cuckoo 33–6, 42–3
curlew 36, 145

dipper 37
diver
    black-throated (N. America:
        black-throated loon, speckled
        loon, lesser imber) 37
    great northern (N. America:
        common loon) 37

red-throated (N. America: red-throated loon) 38
dodo 38–9
dotterel 39
dove 40–1, 82, 153, 154
duck 41 *see also* individual species
dunlin 42
dunnock 42–3

eagle 43–5, 86–7, 174, 177, 200–1
egret, little 45 *see also* heron
Egyptian goose 59 *see also* goose
eider 45–6
  king 46
  see also duck
English partridge 102 *see also* partridge

Feng bird 108, 109
fieldfare 46–7, 145
finch 47–8, 145
  brambling 26
  bullfinch 48
  chaffinch 28, 48
  common redpoll 48
  crossbill 49
  goldfinch 49
  greenfinch 49
  hawfinch 49–50
  lesser redpoll 50
  linnet 50, 82–3
  scarlet rosefinch 50, 135
  Scottish crossbill 51
  serin 51
  siskin 51
  twite 51
  see also bunting

firecrest 51–2
flamingo, pink 113
flycatcher
  pied 52
  red-breasted 52
  spotted 53
fulmar 53

gadwall *see* duck
gannet 53–4
garganey 54 *see also* duck
godwit
  bar-tailed 55
  black-tailed 55
goldcrest 51–2, 55
golden oriole 90–1
golden plover 56
goldeneye 55–6 *see also* duck
goldfinch 49 *see also* finch
goosander 56 *see also* duck
goose 57
  barnacle 20
  bean 58
  brent 58
  Canada 58
  Egyptian 59
  greylag 57, 59
  pink-footed 59–60
  snow 60
  white domestic 60–1
  white-fronted 61
goshawk 61, 67 *see also* hawk
great-crested grebe 62
great grey shrike 148
great northern diver 37
great tit *see* blue tit
grebe 62

black-necked 62
great-crested 62
little 62
red-necked 62
Slavonian 63
greenfinch 49 *see also* finch
greenshank 63–4
green woodpecker 188
grey heron 68–9
greylag goose 57, 59 *see also* goose
grey partridge 102 *see also* partridge
grey plover 115 *see also* golden plover
grouse
  black 64–5
  red 65
  see also capercaillie
guillemot (N. America: common murre) 65
  black 66
gull *see* seagull

harrier
  hen 66
  marsh 66
  Montagu's 67
  see also hawk
hawfinch 49–50 *see also* finch
hawk 35–6, 67–8
hedge sparrow *see* dunnock
hen harrier 66 *see also* hawk
heron
  grey 68–9
  night 69
  purple 70
  white *see* grey heron; little egret
hobby 70 *see also* hawk

hoopoe 71, 88
house martin 85

ibis (Nile bird) 72–3
imber, lesser *see* black-throated diver

jackdaw 73–4
jack snipe 152 *see also* snipe
jaeger *see* skua
jay 74–5

Kentish plover 115
kestrel 67, 75 *see also* hawk
king eider 46
kingfisher 75–6
kite, red 76–7 *see also* hawk
kittiwake 77 *see also* seagull
knot 77–9

lapwing 79–82, 145
lark *see* skylark
Leach's petrel 105
lesser imber *see* black-throated diver
lesser redpoll 50 *see also* finch
lesser whitethroat 184–6
linnet 50, 82–3 *see also* finch
little auk 18–19
little egret 45 *see also* heron
little grebe 62
long-tailed tit 171
loon
  black-throated *see* black-throated diver
  common *see* great northern diver
  red-throated *see* red-throated diver
  speckled *see* black-throated diver

magpie 83–4

mallard 84 *see also* duck

mandarin 84 *see also* duck

marsh harrier 66 *see also* hawk

marsh tit 171

martin 165

  house 85

  sand (N. America: bank swallow) 85

meadow pipit 114 *see also* pipit

merganser, red-breasted 85–6 *see also* duck

merlin 67, 86–8, 89, 200–1 *see also* hawk

Montagu's harrier 67 *see also* hawk

moorhen 88

murre, common *see* guillemot

night heron 69 *see also* grey heron

nightingale 71, 88–9, 164

nightjar 89 *see also* hawk; merlin

Nile bird *see* ibis

nuthatch 90

oriole, golden 90–1

osprey 91–3 *see also* hawk

ostrich 93–4

ouzel, ring 95 *see also* blackbird

owl 95–7

oystercatcher 98–9

parakeet, ring-necked 99

parrot 99–101

partridge 101–2

  common, English or grey 102

  red-legged 102

peacock 102–3

pelican 103–4

penguin 104

peregrine falcon 105 *see also* hawk

petrel

  Leach's 105

  storm 105–6

phalarope 106

pheasant 106–8, 109

phoenix 108, 109, 201 *see also* pheasant

pied flycatcher 52

pigeon 40, 110–13

pink flamingo 113

pink-footed goose 59–60 *see also* goose

pintail 113 *see also* duck

pipit 113–14

  meadow 114

  rock 114

  tree 114

  water 114

plover 145

  golden 56

  grey 115

  Kentish 115

  ringed 115

pochard 116

  red-crested 116–17

  see also duck

ptarmigan 117

puffin 117

purple heron *see also* grey heron

quail 118–20

rail, water 120–1 *see also* spotted crake

raven 29, 121–4

razorbill 124–5

red-backed shrike 149 *see also* great grey shrike

red-breasted flycatcher 52

red-breasted merganser 85–6 *see also* duck

red-crested pochard 116–17 *see also* duck; pochard

red grouse 65 *see also* black grouse; capercaillie

red kite 76–7 *see also* hawk

red-legged partridge 102 *see also* partridge

red-necked grebe 62

redpoll
common 48
lesser 50
see also finch

redshank 125–6
spotted 127

redstart 127
black 128

red-throated diver 38

red-throated loon *see* red-throated diver

redwing 128–9

ring ouzel 95 *see also* blackbird

ringed plover 115

ring-necked parakeet 99

robin 129–34, 163, 169

rock dove 111

rock pipit 114 *see also* pipit

rook 134–5

rosefinch, scarlet 50, 135 *see also* finch

ruddy shelduck *see* duck

ruff 135–6

sanderling 136–7

sand martin (N. America: bank swallow) 85 *see also* house martin

sandpiper 137–42

scarlet rosefinch 50, 135 *see also* finch

scaup 142 *see also* duck

scoter
common 142
surf 143
velvet (N. America: white-winged scoter) 143
see also duck

Scottish crossbill 51 *see also* finch

seagull 144, 151

serin 51 *see also* finch

Seven Whistlers 145–6, 161, 183

shag *see* cormorant

shearwater 146–7

shelduck *see* duck

shoveler 147–8 *see also* duck

shrike
great grey 148
red-backed 149

siskin 51 *see also* finch

skua (N. America: jaeger) 149–50 *see also* seagull

skylark 150–1, 163

Slavonian grebe 63

smew 151 *see also* duck; seagull

snipe 151–2
jack 152

snow goose 60 *see also* goose

sparrow 152–4

sparrowhawk 67, 154–5 *see also* hawk; sparrow

speckled loon *see* black-throated diver

spoonbill 156–8 *see also* heron; little egret

spotted crake 32–3
spotted flycatcher 53
spotted redshank 127 *see also* redshank
starling 159–60
stilt, black-winged 160
stonechat 161
stone curlew 161–2
stork, white 163 *see also* heron; little egret; spoonbill
storm petrel 105–6 *see also* Leach's petrel
surf scoter 143 *see also* duck
swallow 71, 88, 152, 163–5, 168–9
  bank *see* house martin
swan 166–8, 153, 154
swift 168–9

teal 169–70 *see also* duck
tern 170 *see also* seagull
thrush 170
tit 171
  bearded 171
  blue 25
  coal 171
  crested 171
  long-tailed 171
  marsh 171
  willow 171
tree creeper 171–2
tree pipit 114 *see also* pipit
turnstone 173
twite 51 *see also* finch

velvet scoter (N. America: white-winged scoter) 143 *see also* duck

wagtail 173–5
warbler 175–7
water pipit 114 *see also* pipit
water rail 120–1 *see also* spotted crake
waxwing 177–81
wheatear 181–3
whimbrel 145, 183–4
whinchat 184 *see also* stonechat
white domestic goose 60–1 *see also* goose
white-fronted goose 61 *see also* goose
white heron *see* grey heron; little egret
white stork 163 *see also* heron; little egret; spoonbill
whitethroat 184–6
white-winged scoter *see* velvet scoter
wigeon 145, 186 *see also* duck
willow tit 171
woodcock 186–7 *see also* jack snipe; snipe
woodlark 150–1
woodpecker 188
woodpigeon *see* dove; pigeon
wren 42, 163, 169, 189–92
wryneck 192–3

yellowhammer 193–5

NOTES